Into the Tall and the Uncut

John R. Billlings

Edited by Barbara A. Bush

ISBN 978-0984069705

Printed in the USA

Jagdpanzer Verlag

I

# Table of Contents

# Introduction

Federal Republic of Germany:

In the 1970s, I served in the US military as an artillery captain, following the lead of my superiors who had become alarmed over an antiquated, pedantic methodology of target engagement. There were too many inefficient processes supporting the doctrine, and some of the procedures required overhauling. Several of us found a means by which a major linkage could be eliminated, and, a subsequent utilization of more experienced, technically gifted personnel in critical slots saved the lives of thousands of our soldiers in future engagements. Followup from this and other work was the Meritorious Service Medal.

Passion translated to a different venue. This comprised the acquisition of a Yellowstone, Thorofare, wilderness elk-hunting operation thirty to forty miles distant from motorized access, indeed, the most remote wilderness destination in the Lower 48.

In much the same manner by which our group had solved the artillery-acquisition problem, the outfitting organization addressed its logistical constraints, becoming highly efficient. Within a few years, the acquiring of nearly forty head of Mammoth mules, hiring top hands, connecting three camps and achieving unprecedented hunter success, the operation became sustainably profitable. Within a relatively short period, a lifelong goal had been realized. The achievement served as verifiable proof to the contrary of what many permanent locals had claimed. They had said it couldn't be done.

And so, the best was yet to come:

# Foreword, The Monarchy

In twenty-five years of operation, there were only a handful of days in which there was time and opportunity for the proprietor to relax and go hunting. On two such outings, I succeeded in taking elk, and these contributed substantially to winter's providence. The third occasion, one in which there was no success in taking game, proved itself by far the most awe-inspiring and memorable.

It was in the mid 80's, several years following the acquisition of the North Camp, when the business venture began coming together quite well and sustaining profitability. The mule trains were progressing satisfactorily, the colts working well together and assimilating the learning curves of training. It seemed as though everything was starting to run like clockwork. In fact, generally speaking, the organization was incrementally filling the clients earlier on in the respective outings, than in prior seasons, and so there were occasions in which our personnel could take a few days off, with pay, and head for town and refreshment. Sometimes, the clients, owing to demands in their own work, just couldn't get enough of it all, so after filling out, wanted to promptly get back to civilization.

Well, on one of those occasions, back in September of about 1985, it all transpired in simultaneity, and I wound up the sole occupant of North Camp for a couple of days.

The first day of three, if recollection is correct, got spent catching up on chores, changing out pickets, sweeping out the hunter tents, catching up on the firewood supply and tidying up the cook and dining tents. That accomplished, it was not long before thoughts drifted off into the venture department, and visions entered the realm of big bulls in high, isolated basins. Next morning, I saddled up Bandit, and it was not long before we were headed for one of those forty-mile remote drainages. Specifically, this was one rough enough and loaded with down timber, that it never got hunted but once every two or three years.

The timbered regions to the west and north constituted high ridges, golden-brown parks and numerous convoluted draws. These tended to be pervaded by sparse game trails winding amid conifers and connecting intermittent feeding and watering areas. There had been a recent and quite early snow that week, creating a delicately frosted timber and a silver-green continuum. The coldness of the morning lent credence that it might well be a day of non-moon latent activity for the wapiti. For a short time, it was a relief to be free of clients and bustling camps, finding solitude where the mind could recharge.

In the early hours of this first morning out, several elk showed among the meadows that flanked the initial tributary feeding the basin from the northeast. Yet in spite of their sleekness, it was clear that they were younger bulls, attributable as what we used to call raghorns. Experience dictated that the old-timers and more wary six-pointers would prove themselves all the more reclusive, and so it was time to proceed farther up the drainage toward the higher elevations amid the upper end of the basin. An hour later, with Bandit still chomping at the bit to gain altitude, we were frozen by the unmistakeable bugling, resounding amid the upper slides and bouncing off the rimmed walls of the canyon. This was answered, shortly thereafter, by a second. The pair was assessed to be positioned equidistant and triangulated at perhaps four hundred yards range, thereby separated by perhaps a few hundred.

Time to quarter downwind, then ascend to higher ground, thus gaining the options for visibility. Dismounting and dropping the reins, I glassed what apparently constituted a conceivable locale, and succeeded in locating one of the bulls. Minutes later, following detailed perusal, another showed, bugling profusely, and amid frosted breath rising steamlike in crystalline spindrift, began sparring. The antlers crashed together, followed by the pair commencing to, with adeptness, shove one another peripherally around the clearing. The animals were a yellowish gray, with dark manes, their eyes and expressions looking quite ominous. Given the extent of seasonal progression, they sported sleek and heavily haired coats in preparation for the onset of winter. The pair was of better-than-average size, nice looking five-pointers, yet neither manifested as the truly sensational. As the sun rose, the antlers, polished for weeks amid the recesses of dark timber, and in preparation for the annual combat ritual, glittered handsomely. The protractors carried them proudly.

I watched, mesmerized by their antics, as they fiercely assailed one another, locked in mortal combat, and then broke apart, circled and lunged forward again with renewed intensity. Periodic-

3

ally they separated briefly, intermittently withdrawing to opposite ends of the clearing, and then proceeded individually to tear into various saplings, in the process shredding the diminutive limbs to leave subsequently only vestiges of structure. After some twenty minutes of this maneuvering, the pair separated for good, retrograding diametrically opposite one another, finally vanishing like ghosts among the recesses of dark timber.

There existed some probability that a more substantial Monarch might have ascertained and been compellingly attracted to the conflagration. Having assessed that possibility, it seemed best to lend close scrutiny, using the glasses to penetrate the peripheral lanes that pervaded the forest. For the present, it made sense to remain downwind, for if even one of the pair had vectored on compromising scent, both most assuredly would have departed the region, with only a remote and coincidental probability of return. For that reason, I considered it judicious, for investigatory purposes, to decline approaching the chosen battleground, for even a latent human presence is well known to leave a sustainable and compromising scent. Consequently, when the two made their exits, it followed to remain out of sight, reclining amid the deadfall and soft carpet of fresh snow. For some time thereafter, one heard only the chattering of a few squirrels, the occasional overhead piercing of a flying goshawk and a slight breeze rustling the branches of the conifers. It was the splendid concert of the forest. One felt, again, the relief offered by nature, its innocuous absorption of compromising stresses, and became profoundly grateful for the immersion in something greater ... . It always magnified the senses to the point of razor sharpness. One could always scent the elk, and testing the downwind, I made out the barnyard distinctness. Most critically, a full minute after they made their visual departures, one could still ascertain the vibrations as the two faded into obscurity.

In questioning the extent of sensitivity, it was time to go prone and press an ear to the ground ... . There could be no doubt. Only one was moving. A half-minute later, the second resumed. It had paused, no doubt, to check its backtrail.

Time to proceed slowly ... into the breeze, carefully avoiding presumed bedding areas in the midst of dark timber, where the animals were likely to hole up for the majority of daylight hours. Generally, better to seek some of the higher ground, where visibility might provide some clue as to the whereabouts of the object of quest. Early on, one learns the art of detection, of using the binos to search the dark shadows, allowing the light-marshaling refractive index of the optics to enhance one's perception of the subtleties of motion ... the blinking of an eye, an ear rotating forward. One learns to search not for the entire animal, but for a part, something disparate, or for a horizontal line or off-color sector amid what is otherwise commonplace. Often what gets the attention proves to constitute false intelligence, but sometimes what turns up sustains a relevant piece of the puzzle.

It was early on the third day of the outing that I came upon the huge track, perfectly imprinted in a sandbar that diverted a minor tributary circuitously around the timbered edge of a satellite meadow. Upon backtracking, it became evident that that the large bull was master of a substantial group, numbering perhaps thirty head. In light of the abundance of footprints, it proved impossible to definitively follow every step of the leader, but when the track was segregated, there could be little doubt that it represented a bull of tremendous size and weight. Never prior had I encountered elk tracks of such magnitude and penetrating depth.

At the periphery of the upstream side of the meadow existed a concentration of convergent game trails that, gaining in elevation, subsequently disseminated in the direction of darker, heavier conifers. By midmorning, judging from the direction of departure of recently made tracks, it became possible to assess the extended region, beyond the limits of scrutiny, to constitute a possible resting area. It was likely that, by late morning, the bulk of the herd was reclining there, or in a suitable, radially directed, alternate location. Thus, with the breeze presenting the absence of adverse orientation, the choice was to proceed along a transversely vectored wind, for reconnaissance of what presumably amounted to a region of primary feeding.

It was some thirty minutes into this perusal, when a uniquely assailed sapling manifested. Circumvented by an abundance of massive tracks, the location revealed extensive accostment. It was clear that a day or two previously, the main trunk had been severely raked by sharp antlers, and the branches shredded. The resulting broken limbs were scattered for several yards circuitously about what remained of the concentric trunk, badly scarred, the wounds from antler points dripping long rivulets of pitch. Downstream another hundred yards and amid a more diminutive island of conifers, showed another such entity. There, immersed in well-preserved crystalline snow, imminently on the verge of melting, I discovered in isolation from those of the remainder of the herd, multitudes of the same formidable tracks. "Staking his territory."

By that time it was midafternoon, and with the possibility of the herd returning as the sun lowered and shadows lengthened, it was time to implement a plan of action. That boldness would consist of finding a means of gaining sight of the protractor, and preferably one of sufficient duration for a successful shot. That means would constitute laying an ambush.

The trick, of course, amounted to finessing the gain of visual sighting of what might materialize as the trophy class, without being foiled by the vigilant efforts of not only the subject in question, but of thirty or more companions, as well. One thus alarmed would, in all likelihood, raise the entire community, scattering them calamitously and irreversibly in all directions. Further, although the wind direction had not constituted a significant factor for most of the day, as magnitudes had remained diminutive and direction steady, one expected that condition to prove itself short lived. Evening hours invariably offered cooler temperatures, and amid this part of the Absarokas, the altered state habitually meant a few swirling breezes.

It became feasible to set up the ambush location along an upper-apexed extension of the meadow, slightly inside the sparsely timbered approaches. Visibility oriented along the demarcation of intersecting game trails that led from the assessed bedding areas to probable watering and primary grazing topography. The position consisted of quite adequate cover, whose shadows would effect the disruption of any definitive outline, yet provide the optimum access to viable shooting lanes. These constituted predetermined gaps between the conifers. Satisfied with the arrangement, it was time to settle in. One could lean against the blowdown, using it for support among the shadowed bows that shaded the setup, propping the binoculars steadily with the forearms braced, and silently await the vagaries of fate. It was pleasant listening attentively to the surroundings, the music of birds, chattering squirrels and whispering breezes.

Nature's symphony had always been appealing, as it was

6

this late afternoon, but almost subconsciously, one listened to assimilate the rhythms, thus to lend scrutiny should one of the protractors miss a beat. The hideout was geometrically arranged in proper accordance with the incipient angle of the sun's enlightening rays, thus to illuminate the likely approaches from the more heavily timbered sectors. That would mean, conversely, that the view from the standpoint of the approaching would be relatively into the sun, thereby making visual detection of the imposter nearly impossible. It would be imperative, therefore, to remain in the shadows, minimizing movement and sound. That would reduce the essence of detection by the quary to that of scent. It might, assuming the herd had not already departed the region for parts unknown, amount to a critically variable factor, one that was only in part under control of the gunner.

I heard cones hitting the ground, occasionally dropped by squirrels from higher branches. Once, a trio of ravens flew over, sounding their raucous chatter and landing among distant branches along the stream side of the meadow. Their cawing continued intermittently for the next hour, keeping the observer in tune with what might become reactive.

The hunter was startled by the hoof sound that came in off to the right a minute after the easterly breeze picked up, and then swirled about to reorient from the northeast. But the disturbance was remarkably diminutive to be coming from a full-grown elk, and so it was neither dismaying nor surprising when the young buck mule deer materialized, and, catching the latent effects of aberrant scent, bounded off in the direction of better cover. It was notable, the subsequent change in surroundings that followed. The concert abruptly went on hold, and for some time after the buck disappeared, I heard not a sound. Pressing an ear, one caught the fading vibrations of the creature, and it was nearly a full minute before it became certain that they had faded ... . Over several minutes, the harmony of the concert gradually resumed its continuum.

With the sun hanging lower, and the shadows becoming ever more pervasive, one made out the frosty rainbows of spindrift, playing in the last rays. The showers of dazzling crystalline reflections swirled their vortices, and I sat in fascination, contemplating the patterns. *One thinks about what the Creator might have had in mind ... that He perplex a few earthlings with such artistry.*

7

One might have gone deep into thought when, suddenly, he became aware that the concert had halted, once again. Perhaps it was curtain call.

Time to scan the far avenues beyond the proximate timber, noting the sharpness of illumination. A minute later and off the right periphery, one caught the movement, a section of antler extending beyond the bases of a pair of conifers, lowering to the ground as the animal fed along the game trail. A young bull materialized, followed by two more and a pair of cows with calves. Manifesting out of the shadows, they proceeded single file. The calves, exuberant over a timely resumption of horseplay, frolicked around the cows, each chasing the other in randomized circles as their elders proceeded nonchalantly towards the rewards of grazing. It was gratifying to witness Nature in the process of perpetuating its cycles, and the scene generated confidence that perhaps one was on the right track in regard to the quest, itself.

As the forest grew darker, it became evident that the rays of sunlight would be lasting only a few more minutes. The group of seven was disappearing now, and amid the tentative resumption of the concert, the last of the cows filtered into the meadow. Checking the wind, however, it became alarming that the breeze was on the verge of compromise ... and then came the bugling, long deep and gutteral, abruptly answered by another pair. Owing to the intensity of the resonations, they clearly could not have been far off ... perhaps only a few hundred yards. There was an involuntary raising of the hackles, for the final response had emanated with such alacrity that it conceivably represented the power of the sought-after Monarch.

Silently, and concentrating intently, I leaned forward and put an ear to the ground. The vibrations were astounding. An entire herd was moving, creating sufficient turmoil to account for perhaps twenty or more double pair of hooves. It was apparent that the entire procession was headed generally in the direction of the hideout, for the forthcoming vibrations were attaining greater intensity.

It was time to raise up to kneeling, bring up the glasses and scan every detail among the approaching lanes. One could hear them coming, audibly now, breaking limbs and clattering rocks as they ambled along the trails, heading downcountry amid the inception of the nocturnal portion of their cycle. But the breeze was picking up, somewhat, and under the circumstances of its adverse rotation, the aberrant scent would in minutes become detrimentally coincident with the extent of travel.

Damn! It was imperative to move quickly, immediately circling counterclockwise to delay the condemning effects, and at the pronounced risk of detection owing to visual or audible compromise.

Time to break cover, at the crouch proceeding innocuously, orthogonal to the orientation of the wind, silently circling to gain an alternate peripheral vantage relative to the incipient routes of access. Again, the breaking of timber ... this time so close that one might assess the distance at less than a hundred meters. Got to go prone, and raise the level of scrutiny to just above the level of the grasses. A trio of cows materialized, showing intermittently through the lodgepoles and moving unsuspectingly along one of the more distant trails. They were followed by a pair of calves, additional cows, and perhaps at 250 meters, a diminutive bull. For the moment, the wind held steadily, but it felt tenuous, and so one had to make ready to back off into more distant cover and resume circuitous maneuvering, should the whims of Nature negatively readjust.

The cows proceeded slowly, stopping periodically to graze, ever wary of intruders. Always a pair watched while others fed. One had to take care to avoid sudden movements, as elk are noted for their splendid eyesight. I waited several long minutes, watching the group pass to the south, aware that should they continue in the present direction for several more, the lead cow would establish herself within scenting radius of the former ambush position. That prerequisite to chaos would comport to inevitable compromise, and if that were to occur, the quest would most certainly pass unresolved.

By then the breeze had ceased, and through the blades of grass, one could watch, using the glasses, the vapor of exhaled breath as the creatures passed silently to the southeast. The glasses offered nothing further, but the subsequent abrupt and raucous bugling, followed momentarily by the breaking of limbs and crashing of antlers, lent credence to obvious impressions.

The turmoil manifested as a pair of bulls fighting marginally inside the barrier of conifers and just short of the demarcation of visibility. Yet, intermittently, the breeze became more assertive, and ultimately more threatening with a reorientation to the north. Coming to the realization that there existed, in all probability, less than a full minute prior to discredit, one might have assimilated the relevance of the cows paying not the slightest attention to the recent conflagration, nor to their backtrail. Crawling on all fours, it was time to move silently clockwise relative to the sparring, and thus transversely west pertinent to wind direction. It was shortly following the inception of this maneuvering, that it became possible to spot the antlers coming in from the north, undulating rhythmically through the lodgepoles as the bull approached. Time to go prone, and assess the animal by making use of the glasses. Another mature specimen, but clearly not the imperial entity. At 150 yards, the bull came abruptly to a halt, surveying the scene from the edge of cover. Through the grasses, one could watch as the nostrils flared and the vapored breathing slowed. There existed clearly a tension, perhaps from a subtle vibration or an intuition that the condition might somehow be skewed. The bull remained, now anchored like concrete in his tracks, rigidly observant for the minuscule and the suspicious. It was then when, amid the herd, the abrupt bark by the lead cow broke the silence. Moving only the eyes to peripherally assess the lower timber, one could perceive nothing amid the recesses. Certain that any options of further movement were by now clearly out of the question, it was pertinent to redirect scrutiny back to the stationary bull. Now a pair was standing, anchored and ten meters apart, staring precisely in this direction. Confined to remain prone and quite still, it was imperative to sustain the frozen position, in reactive deference to the narrowing options. Then came another piercing bark from down below, this time even more emphatic in nature, and indicative of the threshold.

It was at this point that some shrewdness of calculated apprehensions might, of necessity, have contributed timely finesse then essential to the game. The Monarch, if indeed he existed, was obviously quite savvy, having neither, thus far, shown himself nor uttered any unequivocally definitive resonations. What one had to base any suspicions upon, amounted to the essence of sizeable tracks, massively shredded timber and a sizeable herd. But it was also questionable that a superbly endowed animal would tolerate the presence of rival bulls amid what amounted to territorial manifestation. *In light of these evaluations, one begins to question the absolute certainty of the existence of the entity, at least in the mortal form that had been the object of imagination.*

There occurred, however, a possible means of gaining resolution. The query would come down to an all-or-nothing venture, and would necessarily have to be enacted immediately. With the herd of cows on the verge of explosive vacancy, any of the more wary bulls, would, without doubt, read the inevitably forthcoming message, follow suit and scatter. More than likely the member in question would depart stealthily, and owing to the merits of the shrewdness of that silence, one might never gain definitive evidence relative to the question of existence.

...

*Perhaps one sought that which he only envisioned. He might well never perceive, much less acquire, definitive proof, and all might simply comport to sheer fantasy.*

...

So, what the issue now came down to was that one must somehow smoke out the quary ... and what better means of accomplishing that compulsion than the suggestion of a scandalous appearance of a second Monarch amidst the master bedroom. A dose of well-timed Machiavellian triangulation might just force the hand of the Imperial and draw him out of the lair.

Consequently, it was without hesitation that I pulled the call, one carved two decades prior by an uncle. What manifested was the most raucous, belligerent and cunningly vicious challenge contriveable. The deep, resounding echoes reflected off the conglomerated rims of dark canyon walls, silencing every peripheral concert and menacing proximate conflagration. It was time to press an ear hard against the turf, and strain intently for a clue ... .

And it was a full two minutes later, amid the stillness, that I felt the tread of hooves, coming closer, neither hurried nor hesitant, but steadily confident, exuding the power of ownership. Through the elevated eye, one could perceive the two recent intruders standing rigidly frozen, still focused upon the identical location. They had not moved a single foot. Then amid the final rays of sunset, came the slightest motion, the image of shadowed tips projected against the sizeable blowdown, still held in the last vestiges of light. Incrementally the vibrations faded, and the crowns rotated their wide arc ... and it was overwhelming -- the enormousness of the spread. A spellbinding half-minute later, as the tread resumed, the royal sabres materialized over the diminutive rise, progressively ascending in stature until finally the entire massive structure dominated the setting. Recovering to horizontal vision, the subject ascertained not one audible as the antlers glided silently closer, and the Monarch gained the high ground and came into full view at sixty yards. I reached for the lever-action, intent on silently engaging the hammer to ensure the absence of any metallic giveaway, when from the rear, the restless cows began filtering back in the original direction from which they had come. They were crashing limbs carelessly now, and it was notable, the comtemptuous glare that came from the Monarch, as though annoyed by the mindless intrusion into the more pressing.

Abruptly, one of the pair of bulls pawed the ground as the cows approached. They were bolting then, perhaps eighty yards to my rear, running north along the least encumbered of the trails and seeking denser timber. It became certain that they would take the Monarch with them, and that all would shortly vanish. Thus, there could be not more than a three-second window in which to make a killing shot. The hammer was back. Time to inhale deeply, calm somewhat the quaking nerves, exhale slowly, tense the leg muscles for a readjustment to kneeling position ... . The cows had come nearly alongside, presently, and their hard breathing threatened to disrupt the concentration. The Monarch stood towering and motionless to the front, as the process went into motion ... raising for the shot ... two seconds and he would vanish, the mind raced. But there would be no shot.

The Monarch stood his ground, staring at the intruder, glaring with intensity and authoritative power. In the process of shouldering the lever-action, I halted precipitously, gripped by paralysis. The superb warrior stood, imposingly once pawed the ground, and then redirected vigilance, tracking his charges, as cows, calves and younger bulls lined out and ambled northward, disappearing like specters into denser woods, all the while the Monarch remaining pervasively defiant, holding the terrain until all had safely passed. Then the massive antlers swung around, their arc and spread dominant even in the fading light.

Setting the rifle down, and still stunned by his absolute gaze, I watched as the great bull turned and calmly walked northward into the dark timber, vanishing at the point where the herd had entered.

"Semper talis, Herr Kaiser."

## Chapter 1, Bears, Kamikazes and Train Wrecks

As will be related shortly concerning career-inception episodes, back in the early 1970's I initially worked for several outfitters in Idaho and Montana. Generally they found a wrangler or packer slot, as qualifications relative to guide status were lacking, and preference was to work without supervision, anyway.

On one occasion the process involved signing on with a dude rancher in the Swan Valley north of Clearwater, Montana. He was an old-timer Texan named Fritz. We hit it off after I told him that Grandfather had been Sheriff of Teton County during the Great Depression and bootlegger days, and that he'd once trailed horse thieves back into Blackleaf Canyon and arrested them at gunpoint.

Old Fritz put me to work packing his string of 8 mules. All were black as the ace of spades and twice as ugly. Nevertheless, I became attached to the whole lot of them, and would have, without provocation, been ready to protect all with life, itself, and, on occasion, most certainly did, indeed.

Well, it's not Fritz's string of blacks, but, rather, some of my early 1980's reds enroute to the Thorofare, Wyoming, hunting camps.

Anyways, mules are curious beasts. You either like them or hate them, it seems, and there's very little room among us humans relative to center ground, much less any middle-of-the-road impressions. They are, after all, hybrids, the contrived breeding originally aspired by the well intentioned to assimilate the better traits of both mares and jacks. That's the optimistic rendition. However, sometimes a bit of the worst, or at least the mediocre, perhaps even the horrific, enters the equation, and the genetics start to misfire into chaos. On occasion the wires get totally crossed, and sparks begin to fly, as in both hind feet.

Well, this turned out to be a good bunch, at least for the most part. Forty-plus years later, I still recall their names, as though having met them all just yesterday. There are still prominent visions amid late-night dreams of them lined out on the Holland Creek trail, ears swinging in syncopated rhythm, tails swatting pernicious flies, the packs slung in perfect balance and recalcitrant eyes flashing just a hint of the devil. Oh, those brain boxes weren't born yesterday. I'll tell you, my friend, very few of those long-eared democrats lack savvy, and if you subscribe to fair warning, all of them will test you, sooner or later! There are no exceptions.

Early 1990's: One of three mule trains departing Thorofare camps for the trailheads. We crossed two major passes enroute.

Take the shoeing, for instance. It's a necessity, of course, if your outfit runs rocky trails. In the absence of rock, you can get by with simply trimming the feet, that is, if they are solid and black, and defer nailing the iron until the trails freeze. Then you better get with it quick. Notwithstanding, the best practice is to shoe them all the way around prior to an eight-week season, then reset the whole bunch for what remains. Concomitant, of course, is a timely initial application of borium (hard surfacing).

Now some cowboys and hands planning on hiring on with an outfit are reticent, unless already in dire straits or facing impending hard times, to admit to possessing any skills in the shoeing department. It's been explained, on occasion, that the reason for such men's subjugation of qualifications, lies amid the politics of survival. Some of those cowboys have been around the block, as in Five Card, and in that game the entrepeneur invariably strives to keep that proverbial ace. The fool who commits with all fours might just wind up in the dumpster, jail, as in lawsuit, or worse. Merits of looking to test the "still" water first, for it may run neither "quiet nor shallow."

So, when hiring for the business in Wyoming, I generally asked up front what the skills were. If he proceeded to answer, but clearly omitted some perceived skills, rebuttal was to query the obvious, point-blank. Generally, the response was on the straight and narrow, but evasion raised an eyebrow. Nevertheless, either way, the exercise generally told a great deal about the man.

Well, this somewhat circuitous approach to shoeing mules amid the vagaries of being tested is about finished, serving merely a purpose of laying a little groundwork. So, when it comes to getting iron on those long ears, seems like that hybridization produces a different kind of general temperament from that endemic to horses. A lot of the latter are quite willing, or in short order can be easily trained to accommodate the ritual. The few rough customers can be done using a spectrum of tricks, or, if necessary, the brute-force method. Generally speaking, they are ultimately forgiving, apparently forgetting the negatives within a relatively short time. With mules, experience has been that only a few are initially willing, and if one pushes the envelope of tolerance too far or too fast, few, if any, are forgiving.

With most, you sort of have to con them into going along with the process. One does not force the regimen upon them, but rather appeals to their better sides. If he wants a foot back, you resist a little, but then accommodate. You sort of have to get in tune and read them. Resist a lot, and more often than not the circumstances degenerate into a contest of chaos which you cannot win. If it escalates, and it will do so if one allows it, he'll take his foot, and subsequently give a hind back to you quite abruptly.

Mid 1980's. Twenty head of reds lining out for the Thorofare.

Unlike his cousin, who tends to just haphazardly flail, he'll take aim, and if the bull's-eye is on your behind, that's exactly where he'll connect. If and when you pick yourself up off the ground, he'll likely cant an ear, lay back and taunt you. Those brays were invented for good reason, my friend. In case you fail to recognize their significance, he's offering you a rematch, as in test. It never hurts to heed the language, spoken or otherwise.

So, then, if you conclude that remedy lies in getting tough and throwing the recalcitrant, nailing the shoes on four feet facing north, you are sadly in error. Yeah, every cowboy's done it, thus showing beast and contemporaries who's in charge, here, but that old hen comes back to roost, as well. The long ears, just as those in politics, tend to hold a grudge, and in the bestial version, possess long-term intelligence in terms of recollection, on sight of the perpetrator. Sometimes the endorsement comes even a decade or two later, rubber-stamp applied to the heedless, and blindsiding as in both hind feet, seemingly to the dim-witted, just for the hell of it, but in biding time, aptly administered.

What ultimately works with these mules is simply lots of patience and TLC. Spending time with them over the long trails, the train wrecks, the shoeing, worming, shots, feeding, watering, wrangling them into camp, kicking them out, and a full spectrum of remaining episodes man conducts with these critters, earns their trust and respect.

An easier way to get things done, from four feet in the air.

Unlike within the fast lane of our hurry-up, schlocked-together, plastic culture, there are no shortcuts. The old-timer packers simply paid their dues with these characters, thus learning what was relevant. A cardinal rule is never to show fear, ever.

With these heathens, the place for apprehension is under that stomped-on old hat, or, better yet, in the dumpster. Until you gain familiarity, and this is ongoing, you might expend time and energy observing behavior, on their terms, in the pastures. You can pick out the pranksters, the middle class, the bunch quitters, the grudge holders, the dominant, and those who'd just as soon hang out by themselves, yet not too far from the madding crowd. In any event, and at some point if the line of work is to be taken seriously, you're going to have to join them at close quarters. So, learn to pay close attention to demeanor. They reveal much relating to the realm of intentions. Learn to watch the eyes, ears and whiskers, which telegraph a wealth of information. Those tails switch for good reason, and much of that is neither for swatting flies nor well intentioned. Astute, when in doubt, to stay clear of strike zones. Distracted watching of restless feet is wasted focus. You won't see it coming if a recalcitrant decides to lay you out. Concentrate on what can offer fair warning and reaction time. The ears reflect attention, alertness, attitude and what latently may be forthcoming. The key word is thereafter, as in future tense.

Much of this so-called ground-level awareness gets put to good use on the trail. You've got to work in close proximity to these broomtails. One learns to negate potential consequences of strike-zone entry by pursuing interface mode, as in contact. There, if, somehow, the subject gets offended, he cannot achieve leverage commensurate with his retaliatory effort.

At night, you further refine those interactive skills. Of course, in darkness you won't be able to perceive their eyes, whiskers, etc. But one learns, rather quickly, to listen for swishing tails, and sense those demeanors, as one checks packs, britchens and cinchas amid the pitch black of an October moonless night on the trail. You perceive that their abrupt snorts arise from mental states at variance with those which come out more leisurely. Checking cinchas for proper tension invariably constitutes feeling under them, and this transmits relevant signs as to stress level. Horseback and leading the string, one learns to sense negative intentions, compromises in timing, flaws in lead-rope lengths, balance of packs, misalignment or insidious sliding of pads and literally hundreds of compromising aberrant phenomena which, if allowed to continue unabated, can literally turn to chaos and ruin your night. One learns to sense much of the aforementioned simply through close diligence relative to the lead rope of the lead mule. Through it one senses all of the ten or twelve compadres, and that's a critical link in the equation. So much for introductions.

Nevertheless, regardless of one's approach, these mules, enmasse, hold great potential. Ten of them, seasoned and tied together, will follow the packer to hell and back, over the snarliest of rocky and iced-up trails. Once on a roll, they operate collectively as a finely tuned machine. They will manage in the worst of fallen, rat-haired, fired timber, wind-blown and caving in. Even in deep and drifted snow on marginal and corniced trails, they will proceed without protest on short rations, and for a while on no rations. They are known to sustain their order, enroute and on high passes, through hail, lightning and thunder, while the packer stares, momentarily, in bewilderment at halo's fire between the ears of his saddle horse. Day or night makes no difference. Once conditioned, they are steady, no matter what the vagaries thrown at them by Mother Nature, Father Time or the mistakes of man.

On occasion, I witnessed packers pulling strings of 16, perhaps 18 head, all in sync and wearing impeccable diamonds. Notable that through it all, they seem to ask for nothing more than a square deal. It's up to the packer to make sure it does not come from the bottom of the deck. Trust and respect. Enough said.

Well, ok, back to the black string of democrats. We hit the Holland Creek trail early that morning, back in early September, 1973. Old Fritz had thrown together breakfast at the ranch, and had driven packs, gear and yours truly to the trailhead, thus allowing the concerned to catch a few extra z's. We caught up the stock, saddled and packed up. Fritz waved good luck as we pulled through the gate. Adios!

As we gained a few switchbacks, slowing the saddle horse lent credence to progressively checking the packs and cinchas, both sides and from various angles. Within a few minutes, the inevitable manifested that all was well. A methodology of achieving the essentials while on the fly enhances the sustainability of precision scheduling, and facilitates a few extra hours of coveted rest on the far end of the trail.

So, we made upper Holland and subsequently the pass, pulling over the top into the head of Pendant Creek. A short breather and double-check of all brought us to a rather flat bench among timber where the britchens got tightened a couple notches to accommodate the forthcoming downhill miles into Big Salmon.

The time, in recollection, comes back clearly, with verdant forest and golden tamaracks in fall's splendor. It was a crisp and absolutely cloudless day to kill for. The packtrain, by now mean and lean to the extent that you couldn't drive nails in them, barely sweated over the 9000-foot passes. They travelled machinelike, all the working parts in sync, and with well-balanced packs, sustaining a steady momentum.

But it can all go to hell in a handbasket. Long about an hour or two past midday, we're just past the mouth of Pendant and moving on Big Salmon. There's a section of trail, a hundred yards or so in length, where, some years, one of those unnamed trickles, masses on the surface, and erodes the supporting ground into somewhat of a snarly sort of bedrock chaos. You have to slow the saddle horse and pick a route through all of it, thus to avoid whiplashing the tail end of the train amid the rough spots. Perception and focus are concentrated, accounting for all 32 hooves, as each traverses this maze of rocks, tree roots and blowdowns.

Well, we got through it alright, but in the process of assessing details, this greenhorn failed to account for the greater picture, as in grizzly omitted.

Mr. Grizzly picked one helluva time for intervention. In retrospect, it is obvious that he felt much the same about us. It is apparent that in all fairness and in what amid the tall and the uncut translates to the honorable, Mr. Bruin was more in the ethical right, relative to presence, than we were. After all, man is the intruder, an imposter by manipulation. Nevertheless, no matter neither the fault nor the legitimacy of presence, the combination created one chaotic mess within a very short time ... .

Old griz stands like a mountain, having just pulled the top off of a frazzling, buzzing nest of bald-faced hornets. Jaws snap, canines clack. Glaring eyes burn holes. He's swatting hornets, but incensed, cross-eyed focus is on us. Time to bail off of old Buster, pull the lever action and slam the round. We're still in a foot or so of water, owing to the end of the aforementioned. Mr. Bar is on the far side of a sandy bank about 30 yards off. The lever action whacks a hanging craggy limb, dislodging and sending it down on top of him. Enraged, he sends it flying, in pieces. A couple more salvoes over his head, and trouble bails, blowing the pop stand.

21

Well, in a sense. The griz is apparently intimidated by the facade of force, but not those dang hornets. The baldfaces, their day clearly wrecked, are neither bluffed by the gunfire nor appeased by departure of the marauder. Instead, they redirect retribution to what they deem the proximate threat, attacking enmasse with a vengeance. The author is unaware if any of the readership has encountered the collective wrath of 500 bald-face hornets, but hereby requests that the subscribers allow the latitude of assertion that relative to a string of seasoned, seen-it-all packstock, certainly among the steadiest of the best, there can exist no more potent a source for panic-stricken bedlam!

In a matter of seconds, the entire mass of incensed baldfaces crosses the watery source, descends and proceeds to kamikaze packer and train. There is no place to hide and no defense. Everyone simply has to face the fuscillade. Well, those not-born-yesterday long ears are most certainly not just going to sit there and take it. Several of the baldfaces have flown up Buster's nose and are stinging the hell out of his sinuses. He goes to bucking, as in rodeo, and the packer, remounted, trying to swat the damn things, finds himself dodging blowdowns, snag limbs and trying to steer the ship. Pack train has, of course, set up and can't be held. Now the kamikazes are crawling under the pads of several, and are clearly stinging the hell out of them. Sparks and smoke of the rodeo are starting to look more like the Fourth of July.

Smoke? There's no fire! That's odd. Ah, yes, Jiggs and Buttons are carrying the flour. Of course there's smoke! They're bucking like crazy, smashing the boxes into trees and blowdowns, shattering the structures. Broken boxes, flour and chaos spell flour dust, and it's all over them. Never knew black mules could turn old and gray in a New York second, but it's true. Liquid Larry's is going to be humming on a Friday night when the locals get wind of this one!

Now Sara's got herself jerked over bassackwards by the set up fifth mule, Concho. He's trying to break the line which holds him, creating a stationary target for the kamikazes. But the piggin' string holds, as in flawed, and he simply upends Sara. Now Sara's pack is wedged into the furrowed-out trail, as in anchored. Four legs flail in the air, running to escape the baldfaces, which hover like vultures over the subject in question, ready to descend for the feast. As

22

there is no purchase, those legs  simply flail away in a blurred frenzy.

Moonlight on the White River of Montana's Bob Marshall Wilderness. A fly-by-night packer's paradise!

It's time to bail on this rodeo bronc, as clearly there is business at hand with the grim reaper.  So, I make exit off the left side and land amid rocks and other abrupt entities.  No pick-up man to be found in these parts on a Friday afternoon!  Hobbling on back over to Sara, it's possible to cut the latigos, jettison the pack and pull the snorting hen back to her feet.  Clearly she's declared war on baldfaces, and is kicking at them but finding only blue sky.

Finally, number 8, old Pancho, having a long-standing tendency to kick anything behind, and therefore tied on the rear to save on compadres, is carrying the stoves.  These constitute a set of three folderups, on each side, for the hunters' tents, plus a brand spankin' new cook stove on top, judiciously balanced and split by the diamond for good measure.  Well, he took one look at those hornets and knew what was coming.  For a not-born-yesterday liberal demo, he takes the prize in kicking loose those stoves.  Got the top bucked to hell and the lash cinch busted, with the cook stove now coming down over his behind.  One jump and it's both hind feet in the air, the cook stove majorly dented as in bull's-eye planted, flying in a 30-foot trajectory on collision course for the creek bank. With the oven door ajar, it piles into the rocks and presently assumes more the appearance of discarded scrap.

Next, he goes to work on the aforementioned flopping side packs, plowing them into standing timber. Having seen this elephant before, in 30 seconds he's out of the pack saddle and clear of entanglements. Taking one final askance look at the hornets for good measure, he's high-tailing it up the trail, retrograding for parts unknown ... .

Well, enough adventure for one day, so let's get back to pedantics. It took well over three hours to work around the baldfaces sufficiently to restore a semblance of order out of the mess, and get back down the trail. We pulled into camp late that night, and, of course, there was lots of explaining to do. Just in time to wrangle in a fresh bunch, as in that good old second string, for the meat run back through "paradise" to the ranch. Hope those dang baldfaces cannot see in the dark!

One of the earliest outings relative to the Wyoming operation found five of us packing up near a trailhead called Deer Creek, located forty miles southwest of Cody. Owing to a necessity for stockpiling resources in hunting camp prior to season's commencement, we were taking about twenty head of packstock, plus a couple of spares, along, in addition to our saddle horses. Most of the outfit comprised horses, but one string consisted of five or six well-seasoned mules. The plan was to cover the thirty-two miles distance in about nine or ten hours, the first day, then set up camp over the next several, and finally organize the cargo of extra groceries, horse feed and accessories to facilitate their use over the coming weeks.

Throughout the past several days, all of us had been going in as many directions, thus wrapping up the shoeing, last-minute procurements and other necessary logistical chores. One of the guides, Kelsey, and our cook, Dick, arrived late the night prior at the corrals, joining us with the last of their own horses and turning them out with the remuda. The rest of our group then fed and watered the whole bunch. It was a relief to see the operation finally coming together so well at the last minute, and thus, after a quick thrown-together stew by Dick, we all turned in about midnight, under a nearly full moon, howling coyotes and tall peaks. I recall tracing the lines of that long, lonesome Absaroka trail, silvery in the moonlit ambience, disappearing periodically amid the shadows wrought by imposing spires, and subsequently reappearing seemingly out of nothingness ... connecting man's quest with the nebulous. Drifting off, dreams came and went, and first light dawned with the clatter of rocks, circling stock and lariats finding their marks.

By daylight, we had the whole outfit caught and tied. Dick howled that breakfast was about to get throwed in the fire if we didn't "come and git it quick," so the rest of us tied off those last few ponies and made for the cook wagon ... as in Dick's pickup. Now cowboys pretty much eat breakfast "on the fly," and so we continued the process, rearranging the haltered stock by tying them to alternate corral posts, thus segregating packstock from saddle horses, mules from horses and so forth. With this underway, I started laying out pack saddles, long ago fitted to their owners by name, and organizing packs in pairs, designating pertinent weights and sizes relative to specific animals. Needless to say, Dick's scrambled eggs, coffee, hash browns and toast got gulped amid installments of these rope-jerkin' episodes, with much winding up unavoidably enhancing the contents of the horse feed, itself ... gratuities forthcoming from those eager and open-mouthed, lop-eared friends of the four-legged variety ... .

View of the Deer Creek drainage from our corral.
The trail winds up through the terraces on the right of the canyon.

Amid the frenzy, old Slim hollers from across the corrals,
"Hey, Boss, this one's not going anywheres!"
It's clear we've got one out of the lineup for a while.
Damn, shoestring operation, anyways ... always got to be short on horseflesh, corral space, and long on miles with overloaded packs! When will this greenhorn operator ever figure things out?? I'm thinkin'.
I head on over to Slim and the big palomino named Sidewinder ... the gimping and swelling left shoulder tell the story.
"Got kicked, no doubt by one of the strangers brought in last night," I say.
Slim nods, eyes reflecting concern over the issue, but evincing a sense of relief over, for once, not having to saddle the half cin-

chy "damn heathen" his boss had settled for, owing to details of an earlier horse procurement expedition. We doctor the affliction with linament to curtail the swelling, and proceed to leave him behind with hay and water until return.

A second palomino turns up marginal, with a pretty good welt on a rear coronary band. We'd take him along empty as another spare. One never wins on a tight budget.

Well, we got to throwing those diamond and box hitches and had the whole works packed by about 8:30 AM. Amazing what can get done when a few cowboys manage to get focused! This bunch of amateurs is on the trail well before 9:30 AM, with outrider Willy center positioned, and the rest of us pulling about five head, each.

The packs look pretty good, at least initially. Given the distance and the long climb to the pass, the loads are fairly reasonable, with generally 50 lbs. to a side and a light top of about 20. A few of the feistier broncs carry horse cubes, two bags or 100 lbs. per side, with top packs optional and dependent upon the extent of recalcitrance. That generally takes the fire and "hard to catch" out of the candidates by the time they get to camp.

Well, we line out and head up the initial switchbacks, resting occasionally to accommodate the change in regimen. We can hear Sidewinder at the corral throwing an initial fit over being left behind.

Damn. No doubt should have left Pal back, as well, but this is no outfit for the sick, lame and lazy. Time for Winder to cowhorse up!

As we top over the first bench and disappear from sight, Winder's antics subside, and an attenuating buddy in the string now pays only an occasional subdued lamentation. There is some relief that the former is no longer likely to break down the corral and come hobbling up the trail looking for sympathy. As we top out the second set of switchbacks and enter the ramparts, 1200 feet above the valley floor, all seems to be in relatively good order with the whole machinery in sync and well tuned. A mental break on the march proves itself timely, and it's enlightening to view, from the heights, the local ranches, several among them having wrangled dudes since the 1920's. From the contemplated history, revered for decades throughout volumes written by the original proprietors, one gains a sense of retroed perspectives upon viewing of the relevant topography in the flesh and blood ... Deer Creek, Cabin Creek, Boulder

Basin, Shoshone South Fork and their confluences. At the time, little did I realize that over the next 25 years, illumination provided by those few structures, far below, would shine like a guiding beacon of relief and inspiration at an exhausted end of many a pack train starlit midnight run, solo, out from camp. Historic perusals, amid the rhythmic clickety-clack of ten head, precision ironed, upon nearing the mouth of this enormous and grand canyon of the South Shoshone, I guess. Distant echoes from eclectic founders, mingle

On the trail to North Camp.

... of Valley, the Majo and Triangle X would come back, hauntingly, hundreds of times ... "The light'll be on when ya git in, partner," they all seem to say.

As the string pounds its way through and along the ramparts of an increasingly narrowing canyon, I hear Slim's call for an abrupt

28

halt. "Hold up!---We're losing pack on one of these nags!"

There is no time to more than get the train halted and turn around in the saddle, when "Thar she blows!" Slim's lead pack-horse, Thunder, cuts loose and goes to bucking, scattering a couple of bed rolls, rattling pots and pans, groceries and a shovel from hell to breakfast. The cataclysm all happens in a matter of slow-motion seconds, intermittently frozen in time. Thunder goes to bucking so hard that the max-stressed latigos and lash cinch snap, leaving pack saddle, remnants of the pack, ropes and cover, splat, in the middle of the trail or hanging from the lodgepoles. It takes Slim and Willy at full gallop to finally grab the lead and get that hothead under wraps.

Dammit, anyway, we should have weighed out those loads the night before and taken the guesswork out of our greenhorn lazy bedridden habits. Perfection is the standard prior to hitting those trails, and such lessons, among many more timely, would prove themselves invaluably relevant for acquisition of this snorty, rope burnin' trade. Those scales would repeatedly make liars out of boy scouts and wannabes, and horses the likes of Thunder would re-mind us that "if the cowboys can't git it right the first time, we'll buck it off and start over!" Anyway, a few bruises, but no harm done that cannot be fixed. We cobble the busted lash cinch back together with a leather punch, driving hammer, as in shoeing, a few rivets, latigos resurrected with baler twine lock-threaded through shredded holes. Within twenty, we are gathered up, repacked and back in business.

Several uneventful miles pass, the grade climbing gradually, culminating with a few of the unacquainted colts and grudge-holder types starting to kick a counterpart to the rear, or biting hell out of one to the front. We halt a couple of times to rearrange the chaos, finally getting the semblance of a reasonable pecking order in place on the third effort. This ends the insurrections for a while, as we take on a steeper section of Firebox Hill.

About halfway up that set of switchbacks, we come face to face with the Castle Rock outfit, bringing out their last summer pack trip. The whole crew has laid over in Freezeout Basin at the upper end of Butte Creek, just west of the demarcation between Deer Creek Pass and eastern extremities of the Thorofare Country. Their dudes look well rested and seem to appreciate the break in schedule. All of our group are well acquainted with most of the Castle Rock hands, so we work the strings into proximity, palaver a few greetings, give a quick adios and drive on.

We climb steadily for the next several hours, eventually reaching the upper switchbacks and the pass without incident. It is grand witnessing simultaneously the Shoshone Basin and the Carter Mountains to the east, with the Thorofare Buttes and the Yellowstone country stretching southwest, nearly all the way to Jack-

Thorofare Country and Butte Creek, as seen from Deer Creek Pass.

son Hole.

We've ascended to well over 10,000 feet, a climb, in eleven miles of trail, of more than a mile in elevation above the corral and level of the South Fork. A most sobering revelation comes from sighting quite substantial quantities of broken-up horse gear, progressively aging since the 1930's owing to weather and exposure, which have accumulated over subsequent decades of train wrecks. We are witnesses to torn-up pack saddles, shattered panniers of wood and fiberglass, shredded britchens, breast collars, shattered skulls, and broken horse bones. Far below, at the inception of the headwaters stands the massive graveyard, where snowslides, avalanches or the bad habits of careless and hapless packers have ended with tragic consequences. Hollowed eye sockets staring vacantly from bleached-out skulls evince stories of horror only tersely revealed in subsequent whispers by inebriated cowboys bearing witness amid delerium at closing time on long nights in the dead of winter. The inviolate debuts at demarcation with the sacrosanct.

So, we drop off the pass on the windward side, heading into upper Butte Creek meadows and the Thorofare. The terrain and conditions change abruptly from rough, austere, rocky and quite dry to more rolling, verdant mountains, full of parks, meadows, the vitality of fast-flowing streams and abundant wildflowers. One cannot help but marvel at the esoteric nature of the place which evinces more the idyllic qualities of Yellowstone than those which constituted even the subjects of enchanted childhood dreams.

Through timber and tall grass, fit for kings and cowboys, alike.

The stock now seem to concentrate less on the precision of foot placement and stretch out somewhat to make better time. Clearly, the hay burners have their minds on all that tall grass in the meadows along the creek above camp. Now the cowboys kick back for an occasion to disseminate the contents of a number of saddle bags, as in several bottles of jack. These are distributed by the out-rider, who does his best to obfuscate the process by avoidance relative to scrutiny by the outfitter. Well, sacred might well be sacred, but, aw hell, it's always Saturday night somewhere!

Anyway, all is well with the pack strings, and the cargos, so we pound out the miles through paradise full of endless meadows, tall grass and mountain streams, long shadows of evening covering the trail. We hit the Forks and give the stock a long drink. Shortly into the process, a bull moose holed up along the bank of the river, snorts abruptly, rises up and heads downstream for parts unknown. In sync, twenty-five pairs of ears come up to radar focus as he clatters away through the rocks. Then, nonchalantly, the heads drop down for more water.

The march continues, and we make good time.

Just before dark we hit the big meadows at Badger Creek and turn upstream, entering the final leg toward camp. We halt to check the cinchas, readjust britchens and generally look over the packs. A full moon is appearing in the east, and the early stars are just starting to show. About a mile off, up near the park line, a bull elk sounds, the intonations raising hackles, reminding that opening day is shortly forthcoming. Slim, riding first to the rear of the initial string, gives a holler, pulling up adjacent in the clearing.

"Hey, boss, that's the first of this fall! Probably a lone bull on the prowl, looking for a fight on a Saturday night!"

"I'll drink to that."

He pulls the half-empty bottle of jack from the saddle bag and hands it over. I take a pull and return it. "Here's to the war and Valhalla!"

Smiles exchanged over the prospects ... abundant game, a full season and prosperity coming ... and home, once again, amid paradise.

"Well, let's go to camp," I say.

We line out and head up the creek. The moon is noticeably higher, now, the sky darker, and the stars more prominent. A meteor, bright green, shoots in slow motion halfway across the hemisphere, finally shattering into a shower of sparks. One cannot help but contemplate the thoughts of the paleolithics marveling for the first time at the sublimity. Clearly, the esoterics of the issue haven't changed in three-quarters of a million years ... yet, relatively speaking, only man has.

"Hey boss!"

"Hey what?"

"Hey boss ... hold up!"

Silence.

"Kelsey's nowhere in sight!"

I halt for what seems like several minutes. It is cooling off fast, and the impatient packhorses are starting to dance, stomping, eager to make camp and get turned out on the abundance of fresh grass and water.

"Any luck?" I holler back.

"Dick's going back to look for him."

"Alright, let's get going ... . Got to get these heathens unpacked. I'll go back later if necessary."

We ride the last 45 minutes in relative silence, breaking a few new-fallen limbs that weren't on the sparse trail the previous November when we pulled out. Finally, we clatter across the creek for the last time and proceed up the bank to the timbered park and our campsite.

Well, twelve hours on the trail is clearly no speed record, but not so bad for a first of the fall season "pack in" with some of these soft horses.

We tie up that snorty bunch of nags to trees and a few stout hitching rails left up last fall for the purpose. Within about twenty minutes the three of us have nearly half the stock unpacked, with the loads categorically segregated and grounded in a long line behind the hitchrails. It is about that time that Kelsey's horse, Stranger, shows up, making time, saddled and dragging one rein. He's got kind of an aberrant look about him, bewildered like, and appears afflicted with a nefarious case of the "look behinds." No sign of Dick or Kelsey, so with my endorsing nod of approval, Willy climbs on his horse and takes off back in the proper direction.

"Touch one off if there's trouble!" I shout as he departs.

Slim and I finish with the unpacking, cover the loads and unsaddle the packstock. We stack the pack saddles and pads, bell the horses, feed a sack of cubes to them in the meadow and with our saddle horses run the bunch up the creek. Upon return to camp, I'm picketing the night horses while Slim builds a fire and gits coffee goin'. Intermittently, we hear them coming.

...

"Rye whiskey, rye whiskey, rye whiskey, I cry
If a tree don't fall on me, I'll live 'til I die!"

...

The melodics of Willy and Dick bellering the old Tex Ritter classic are a memory to kill for, yet Slim and I are perplexed as to why Kelsey hasn't joined the concerto. It turns out that would prove itself impossible, for as the reconnaissance boys proceed to relate, Dick had found him face up in one of the lower meadows, surrounded by his faithful string of grazing horses. Several had managed to step over their leads and "were fixin' to cause one helluva wreck." As Dick finally managed to untangle the string and tie the bunch separately to trees, Willy showed up and the two succeeded in "sobering" Kelsey enough to git him on his feet, but, unfortunately, of course, there was no pertinent saddle horse to be found.

"Wound up in camp," Willy chimes in presently, gulping the coffee.

So, they decided to repack the swaggering, lurching Kelsey, mumbling some incomprehensible lyrics of Bob Wills' San Antonio Rose, over Willy's saddle horse, Pancho, securing the lost, but newly found cargo, with a double diamond to kill for. And that, my friends, is the pathetic condition in which Kelsey, Dick, Willy, a couple of saddle horses and the last five head of packstock arrived in Badger Creek hunting camp, around midnight in late August of 1979.

We pour old Kels out of the saddle, unpack the string, and soon all five of us are sitting around the fire drinking Slim's coffee. Dick is fixin' to fill us full of "end of the trail stew." Finally, it's time to get details of the recent adventure.

Kelsey laments, tentatively, that none of it was his fault ... that the high altitude and the jack had unexpectedly conspired about the time the moon came up! He had stared up at the moon, and damned if it didn't start dancing around and eventually begin going in circles. The harder he concentrated to ward off the inevitable, the worse it got, until finally he got dizzy and fell off his horse. He tells how he started dreaming that he had kicked the bucket and swears he had gone to heaven, and that "free-flowin'," but somewhat warmish beer was "just everywhere!" But then Dick interrupts and says that when he had first arrived on the scene, the horses had gotten too close to Kelsey, and had started, and were fixin' to continue, while mindlessly grazing, pissing all over him, and that that had constituted the initial emergency.

With that, Slim and Willy now abrubtly proceed to drag Kelsey off in the direction of Badger Creek, downstream and far from the spring that was our drinking water supply, for a good dousing.

"Time to stop asking questions," I mumble.

Nodding in the firelight, Dick smiles briefly, stirring our supper. The aroma is killing both of us as we wait for the boys to return.

The stars and moon shone brighter, then, and I still remember the fading of coyotes howling and of an old bull elk answering. It would not take much more to keep oneself content.

# Chapter 3, Ace of Spades

For nearly forty years, it has kept me awake at nights, wondering about a strange bear we shot in camp. Dick and Slim had caught him pirating an elk carcass hanging off the meat rack. Bears frequently attempted to steal the quarters we used to store at that location, but this bruin was unique. In possession of definitive characteristics of both the americanus and horribilis species of the genus Ursis, he appeared to be part black and part grizzly. Perhaps he was a hybrid.

It has proven equally perplexing as to how he managed to survive the antiquated, massive hole and outrageous wound in his skull.

We were booked full that season back in about '79, and our first few September trips had four hunters, apiece. Slim and Kelsey guided two, each, while Dick cooked and Willy wrangled. The elk bugled profusely the second trip, with several good herd bulls sounding off early and late within walking distance of camp. Owing to a full moon, the old-timers usually went at it all night, as well, crashing their antlers and bugling, sparring away, and as a result none of us got much in the way of sleep. In the mornings, everyone was up, bright eyed, by 2:30 or 3:00 AM, drinking Dick's overpowering coffee, waiting on the "witching hour," when hunters and guides could optimally leave camp, silently climb the ridges and thereby minimize the spread of one's own scent. Consequently, it was only a few days before we had two pretty decent bulls on the ground.

It is well documented that elk, themselves, possess a keen acuity of perception in that department, and many a careful approach by humans can be botched in a few seconds by a momentary change in wind direction. Even a slightly aberrant breeze carries an element of chaotic sabotage. For in the absence of its realignment, or pertinent compensation for on the part of a careless participant, a mere few moments brings compromise, and a fading of the quest's ghost into dark timber. And so, the enigma of pursuit becomes an artful one of elevated vigilance and awareness, at nearly second-nature instinctive level, relative to mitigation of compromising wind currents, with the stalking refinements assimilating mastery of maneuver by obfuscating encirclement. Time in the lairs of the monarchs must therefore be optimized.

Temperatures were running into the low 70's by midday that late September, and by the time those front and hind quarters hung in the shade on the meat rack behind camp, it was decision time. I therefore set out, midway though the outing, on a freezer run, packing the two bulls and a buck mulie to the trailhead. The option of covering the thirty-plus miles at night meant cooler travelling, and, of course, a more accommodating processor.

The all-nighter proved uneventful, save for the magnificent moonlit views of the Thorofare Buttes and Deer Creek canyon. A pair of old, raucous bulls bugling away on Woody Ridge lent credence that this year the rut might well continue to the first week of October. A pack of coyotes below the Buttes seemed to answer them, providing entertainment while hunting mice as the lone rider passed.

At 2:00 AM, and from ten thousand feet, nine miles of Deer Creek, Kingfisher Peak and the Carters shone like silver, their reflections among oceans of stars amid the galaxies of infinitude. The stock seemed mesmerized by the enormousness of it all, proceeding as though calmed by the eternal. Clearly, they were, for treading like soldiers on a comfortable march, timely arrival at the corrals came not long before daybreak ... .

Resting the stock a day before packing up to return to camp, I drop off the quarters at one of the local processors in Cody, then reload the empty panniers with horse feed. Next day, the return trip goes in without a hitch, except for when, shortly after sundown, the saddle horse, Chief, snorts loudly and halts abruptly on the main Thorofare trail. In the waning light I make out the shadow of the massive grizzly, thirty yards ahead and standing on all fours, assessing us. Instantly, he is gone, scrambling through deadfall and breaking limbs. As the string picks up his scent, there are brief fireworks, necessitating some rebalancing of packs and retightening of cinchas.

Finally, upon reaching camp two hours hence, getting unpacked, the stock fed, watered and turned loose, I'm in for a surprise at the cook tent. There is hot coffee on the stove in that location, and it's time for indulgence. Next door, in the dining facility, the cook and two guides are conversing, and evidently we are facing decision time. With Dick subsequently warming up supper and the gunners gone to the late-night racks, Slim and Kelsey now finally come out with the story.

Apparently, the morning I was in town reorganizing for the return, Slim and his hunter scored on a nice five-point. They dressed and quartered the bull, returning to camp for a quick breakfast and some packstock. The retrieval had been straight forward, and by early afternoon the bull was hanging on the meat rack. The whole camp, by then, was on cloud nine, with three of four hunters filled and four more days for Kelsey and his gunner to finish the job. The splendid weather would mean time to relax, play cards, take photos and go fishing.

A small front came through later that evening, bringing a little rain and cooling things down. Along with that came chaos, as Dick, being an especially light sleeper, heard ominous sounds out at the meat rack. Holding a flashlight and rifle in hand, he came face to face with a growling bruin, snapping his jaws and proceeding to make supper out of our elk. Looked like an old black to Dick, who then made tracks for the guide's tent and woke up Slim. In the drizzle, the critter certainly looked dark as the Ace of Spades to both of them, so Slim dropped him with two shots from his trusty 308 lever action. This, of course, woke up the whole camp, lanterns were started, and the scene became abundantly illuminated.

Everyone was convinced the animal was a large, old-timer black, weighing an estimated 300 pounds, missing the telltale grizzly hump. The claws were blunted and subdued, failing to extend beyond the prints left in the mud. He also possessed a hideous scar of major proportions below the right eye. In the morning Slim and Willy skinned the bear, while Kelsey guided the unfilled hunter:

Finally, Slim tells me that they had hung the bear pelt in the sun off one of the hitchrails. Over several hours, the hairs began to dry out some, and although they had retained a definitive blackness, the ends began to assume the character of silvertips.

"Hm, that's perplexing," I note. I had never encountered a silvertip black, but perhaps he was just getting old and gray. Still, no hump and short claws pointed unequivocally to an identity of black bear, and not grizzly.

Well, then Slim and Kelsey show me the skull, now, of course, absent the hide and, most notably, the scar. I've seen a fair number of bear skulls over the prior years of guiding and hunting, yet never have any given a case of the grips like this one does. There is a massive hole at least the cross-sectional dimension of a silver dollar which, through calcification, has deformed the lower extremity of the right orbit and has eliminated the corresponding sinus region of that side. Further, calcification has significantly contributed to irregular extensions of the skull structure, thus rendering the same attributable to neither that of horribilis nor to that of americanus. It has further contributed to the ghastly scarring found on the hide. It is apparent that this is a very old wound. What is amazing is that the animal had survived it.

Next day, we look over the hide several times, and as the follicles continue to dry out, they progressively assume more prominent silvertip traits by nature. We are baffled.

A day later, Kelsey fills his gunner with a fine six-pointer, and consequently the former and I pack up the hunters and depart for the trailhead. In the meantime, Slim meets the Game Department, which shows up in camp, and whose representative, in spite of the absence of convincing features, claims the bear is a grizzly. Months later, Slim pays a modest fine, and the issue is forgotten.

But the real intrigue is with the old wound. The issue is haunting, and I cannot sleep over the torment. It is baffling how a bear might have sustained such signatures. I ask around some of the contemporary camps in the neighboring drainages, and pursue some bar talk and gossip in town. No one seems to have any credible ideas.

It is late in the dead of the following winter when I receive a phone call from a friend of Kelsey. In reference to the "bear episode," he advises to give Jensen Outfitting a call.

Evidently, years ago they had hired an old-timer guide who used to work in my camp several outfitters prior. Apparently, he had related that in those days, he used to sleep in the cook tent, thus to hold the fort relative to possible "furry nighttime intruders." He carried a "sawed off twelve," double-barrel, loaded with rifled slugs. On a late-night vigil back in the sixties, he had pulled down on a grizzly standing on the dining table and a few feet from his cot. He had let fly with both barrels, knocking the bear head over heels off the table. Evidently, the animal recovered enough to vacate, leaving abundant blood and bone splinters.

Next morning, the crew had given pursuit, but no cigar. No

one since has offered further knowledge, thus never has there been resolution: only conjecture. Consensus is that the wounded bear had holed up in some dark, unassailable timber and undoubtedly perished. Still conjecture, however.

But don't the antisocial habitually return to their own scenes? Perhaps our hybrid cross Ace of Spades provides an answer of his own ... more conjecture ... and, with distraction, I'm searching still.

## Chapter 4, Smokin' Tom

The forthcoming is cobbled together like patchwork, based in part upon clientele-offered details of hunting adventures with Tom Schmittmann, in conjunction with those of the participant author.

Back in the early 1970's, long before purchasing any hunting camps, I worked some summer and fall seasons for several outfitters, outside the home state, to acquire experience. New country and unmet folks were always intriguing. They proved themselves good teachers, as well. One such character hired me in early September, sight unseen, following a couple of letters and a short phone conversation.

A week later, he called back with an abrupt, "Meet me at the corrals on the Middle Fork."

By the Middle Fork he referred to the center tributary of the Salmon River, which exited the Yellowjacket Mountains forty miles west of North Fork, Idaho. Next morning, I threw a few clothes and an extra pair of old, runover boots into a duffel bag, grabbed the trusty rifle, and departed the Darby home place for the aforementioned. The misfiring old-timer pickup made good time, and pulled in about 7:30 AM.

I couldn't have failed to recognize Marlboro Tom, his local nickname, a tall wire with a silver belly jumped-on hat, leaning against one of the tack sheds, left boot perched on an adjacent corral rail. As he reclined in the shade, a couple of shoers were ganged up in the nearby sunlight nailing iron on a protesting Appaloosa gray. There were about thirty head in the corrals, the broken and missing rails indicative that the structure had seen better days. Most of the stock looked a bit lean for early fall.

I pulled up, cut the motor, and walked up to Tom. "I'm yer man."

"Tom Schmittmann."

"John Billings."

It was clear that he was looking askance at the 50's banger while sizing me up.

He looked the part ... silver, ten-gallon on top, tall boots, about 6' 2", and pearl buttons. Chewed snuff part time, the rest of the time smokin' coffin nails.

"Ya been packin' much?"

In spite of previous conversations he apparently wanted better proof, I thought. Time to reiterate what we'd already discussed about time spent in the Bob Marshall and the Beartooths.

"Well, what the hell do them Montanians know about anything, anyway?" Out came the chaw, and fumbling with the pack and matches, he lit the cigarette. "Damn podunk cowboys over there think they got all the answers."

Silence seemed to lend credence that Idaho was not making much of an impression ... . "Can you shoe horses?"

"We've had this conversation before ... . What have you got for me?"

He stood up, then leaned on the top rail of the corral. "Ya see that sorrel-lookin' heathen over there ... one with the bald face? He needs shoes. Show me what ya can do."

I gave a two-fingered rather sarcastic boy scout salute, walked over to the shoers and made introduction. They were Charlie and Bill, hands who had worked several years for the outfit, and seemed decent enough. I asked Bill about the baldface. He stood up from the shaping, walked over and shook hands. Quietly, he offered, "He's testing you ... always uses that renegade on the new help. He's good on the fronts, but watch him on those hinds. Likely, he'll settle in, then jerk away and blindside about the time you start in with the rasp. If he was mine, I'd tie him up. Holler if you can use some help."

"Thanks. Where's some tools?"

By that time, Charlie was bringing an old rusty set and motioning to an anvil next to one of the hitchin' posts.

...

After catching the baldface and taking a single wrap on the rail with the lead, it is time to get acquainted with this character. Clearly, Baldy is not overly fond of folks, his eyes and that look about him betraying the ulterior notions. The same might be inferred about Tom, who seems possessed of rather twisted inclinations. It is as though two of a kind had met, and there is pause to consider the symbiosis.

Well, the work on old Baldy takes over an hour of going steady and careful, deliberately keeping the feet diminutive and comfortable. When it comes to the hinds, a pedantic and low-key process of "creeping around" seems to achieve an acceptable balance. A few occasions of feeling surfacing vibes of those blindsiding contemplations receives compensations in the formats of lesser incremental stresses by installment.

When the job gets finished, a brief perusal of the judiciary quorum reveals all three together, leaning on the rails, staring. In a few moments, Charlie clears his throat rather loudly and calmly states, glancing in Tom's direction, "Well, that's a first ... . Uh, Tom, maybe you better put this guy on the payroll."

"Yeah," Bill sounds off. "Maybe he'll be able to get Badger and Petunia done without a circus, as well."

Finally, relieved to have managed to get past old Baldy, it's time to move on. "Maybe just got lucky, this time, fellers. Which one is Badger?"

By now, Tom has already caught him. Bringing him, he hands over the lead. "A whiskey sour if you can get him done without a footrope."

Well, no whiskey, this time, but Bill, Charlie and I gang up on that snake, and two hours later, we have iron on him. It is no perfect job, but the shoes will stay on until they wear through on those rocky trails late in the coming fall. By dark, we have Petunia and nearly all the rest finished, as well.

So, Smokin' Tom comes forth and says I am hired, and that we'll be going up the trail, a day later, with the first group of clients. Reminding him that that issue had already been decided over conversation the week prior, makes no impression.

Next night, the four gunners arrive, and old Tom has them booked into some shady rest in the town of Salmon, where they are all assigned to one room, apparently with two double beds. These guys are from Georgia, construction workers from Atlanta, and they seem pretty out of sorts in the parking lot when they bring us their duffel.

Bill and I weigh out the packs, balancing the loads, while Charlie helps them organize the remainder of their gear. All the while Tom collects their fees, and after a short explanation detailing that he will meet them early for breakfast, departs in his pickup to "finish up the last details." Just before Tom leaves, the apparent leader of the group, a fellow named Jack, asks about the accommodations in camp. He says all of his group want to know what the hell the damn sleeping arrangements are going to be. Will four of them have to sleep, two to a cot, for ten days up there, also?

Tom responds that there's goin' to be single bunks in the tents, but that it wouldn't be a bad idea if the hunters brought a few extra matress pads and rain tarps, as well. Finally, a second hunter named George raises an eyebrow and asks, "What the hell is that supposed to mean? We've all got our own rain gear. Are there any roofs left on those moldy tents in camp?"

So Bill, Charlie and I load the two trucks with all the hunter gear and packs and head back up the North Fork to the corrals, where we spend the night. Tom plans on having breakfast, the following morning, with the hunters and then bringing them to the trailhead where, hopefully, the three of us would have the horses saddled and the packing well underway ... .

It turned out, however, that next morning we got the saddling and packing done long before Tom and the hunters showed up. Evidently, unknown to all, there would transpire quite a number of delays, some expected and some not. The first occurred when it came time to pay the bill for breakfast. The "boss" said they'd all have to "go dutch," to save money for picking up the rest of the groceries. Getting that sorted out took quite some time, for the gunners had "accidentally" packed their wallets and all the money with the duffel. Finally, the waitress came up with an IOU loan to the outfitter with remuneration and tip promised by the end of hunting season. That left the hunters rolling their eyes and with "I told you so" expressions for each other.

Next stop was the local grocery, where Tom had a couple boxes of grub waiting for pick up. The checkout lady offered the butcher shop service of slicing the five blocks of yellow cheese for two bits, apiece, but Tom said, "Hell, no, we'll do that up in camp!"

Then came several more stops at the hardware store, lumber yard, tack shop, another local restaurant and two bars to pay, from the demeanors of several of the attendant proprietors, evidently "delinquent" bills ... then another at the filling station for two quarts of oil to feed the one-lunged, coughing pickup they were all riding in. Amid a deluge of choice and chiding comments, Tom pulled into the bank parking lot, raised the hood and poured the two quarts down the hatch ... followed by a quick "drop off" in the main office.

Finally, all systems are go, save for one final pick up of a horse trailer and three more head, "borried" from a neighbor. That accomplished, horses, more gear, groceries, dual-cab pickup and trailer, outfitter and consternated gunners are headed for the North Fork. All is well.

But dammit, anyway, about twenty miles out from the corrals, danged if a rear on the pickup and an old baldface on the trailer don't simultaneously give up the ghost. Tom gets out, locates the only spare, throws his jumped-on old hat into the gravel, and adds insult to injury. Then, suddenly, he puts on this enlightened look, gets "head up," again, raises an eyebrow, and hauls out an old chain and the handyman jack from the tool box. By this time two of the gunners are lending a hand with the spare pickup tire, so Tom commandeers George, and they off-load the horses. They hand off the leads to Frank, and then proceed to jack up the trailer. "No spare for the SOB? ... we'll see about these "two bit" chicken-livered, foul neighbors!" After chaining the jacked-up axle and frame, and with George holding steady, the handyman and the crowbar-jammed tightened chain, Tom returns with the vise grips, dug from the bottom of the glove box. Then comes a bit of finesse; George is instructed to carefully release the pressure, the device holds and all is well in paradise. Then, without incident, the spare is applied to the disconnected pickup, the trailer rehitched and the horses loaded. Finally Tom, with a grin of satisfaction, announces, "Boots and saddles, gents ... we're back on the trail!" They all get in, and with an initial banging around of horses, and a lurching, backfiring rig, the contraption continues on to destination without further incident.

They pull into the corrals relatively intact, save for the smoking, oil-starved pickup. Yet, except for the 4 head remaining, the place is deserted: no hands, and the transport is up the trail. Back in those days, cell phones were only a figment of imagination, so we've left Tom a note:

...

"Waited 'til noon. Headed for camp. The boys and 26 head."

...

"Well, dammit! Thinkin' every minute, those pikers! Hell almighty! These 'borried' renegades better be decent!"

With two of the four left, packstock only, it didn't take rocket science Tom long to figure out that the three borried were going to have to be rideable. So, he goes to packin' the extra loads of grub, etc. on two of the former, and throwing his own saddle and a padded one on the pertinent remaining. By this time, the hunters, standing around observing, are starting to snap to that three of them are now going to have to ride the borried ones still in the trailer. Presently, these have started ominously kicking and banging around, impatient to end their confinement.

Tom walks over, clearly contemplating the next move, opens the way out, and grabs the leads, handing them off to the hunters. Those horses are showing all the signs, among others, as though having not been trailered much. The gunners, of course, having not totally been born yesterday, are picking up on a few of the inferences.

Next, old Tom pulls riding saddles, pads and tack from one of the sheds and proceeds to saddle the first. Can't even get close with the brush. "Aw, hell!" So, he ties up the others to the corners of the trailer, then proceeds with the first inside the corral, snubbing that cayuse to the center post. As he begins with the brush and pads, that wild-eyed heathen starts to bucking and throwing a god-awful fit. "Hey, Don, throw me yer jacket! ... Jack, there's a long, fat rope in the tack shed. Bring it, would ya?"

So, Tom ties up the offside hind, then proceeds to brush and saddle ... but High Ball will have no part of that and starts dancing on three legs. Then comes the jacket, putting High Ball in the dark. Tom saddles, bridles and climbs on the snorting heathen.

By now the clients, amid varying degrees of the incredulous, are staring at each other, and proceeding to question the viability of the venture.

"He can't be serious ... . You mean we are going to be riding these things?? ... . Uh, Tom, isn't there another way?"

"Alright, George, when I tell ya, pull the blindfold!"

In the meantime, Tom leans forward and releases the lead, sustaining loosely the reins, then disengages the footrope, talking calmly to High Ball, repeating that everything is alright.

"Alright, George, come up slowly and lift the blinder."

That accomplished, Tom motions him back, the other hand sustaining the reins. Further loosening incrementally, he nudges High Ball in the flanks, "Easy, boy, easy now ... it's alright."

Suddenly, High Ball jump starts, crow hopping a bit, but then Tom holds him somewhat in check. They make a few rounds of the corral, Tom redirecting the energy peripherally, and talking to him.

Twenty minutes of this and Tom gets George's attention, motioning him to open the gate. That accomplished, he proceeds to ride back towards town, down the old dusty road. Thirty minutes later, they're back, High Ball snorting and Tom grinning.

"Well, save for the bit, he's graduated. We'll take care of that when we git to camp!"

However, the gunners are having other thoughts. On the verge of mutiny, they've appraised the situation and want no part of these 'knotheads with small brains.'

"We're not going up your trail, Mister," asserts Jack. Don and Sam echo that they would not be spending their hard-earned money for a rodeo on the trails of Idaho.

"Well, gents, the rodeo's over. I'll ride High Ball, lead the two packhorses, and Jack, you take that black, my personal horse, Gunsmoke. He and that sorrel, Red, are bombproof. ... Don, why don't you ride him?"

"What about Sam and George?" Jack snaps, still skeptical.

"The two tied to the trailer," Tom responds, dismounting from the spinning-away High Ball.

He recatches High Ball, tying him to a stout corral post outside. "Well, let's see about the last two."

"The same circus all over again, huh?!" snaps George, still reticent over having faced High Ball's glare at close quarters, up front and personal. "I'll be damned if I'm riding either of those two," motioning for effect, by thumb, toward the horse trailer.

"Ever play Five Card?"

Silence.

"Wal, I've got an ace and a hundred dollar bill on each says you can climb on and ride 'em. ... give me twenty minutes, apiece."

More silence ... then, "Ok, mister, but you better pay or get lynched if it doesn't work!"

So, inside the corral, Tom saddles Elmer, hitches the bridle and climbs on. In a few minutes, he's rode the kinks out, heads out the gate and down the road. He's back shortly with that lantern-jawed smile. "Graduated."

Same with Rooster.

So, with Jack in the lead on Gunsmoke, Tom right behind on High Ball, handling the two packstock, Sam, George and Don pull up the rear. They're headed up the Middle Fork trail in search of adventure. It is 5:30 PM, and it isn't pretty. Nevertheless, all are on point, fully awake for what might well be coming. Smokin' Tom, fully aware that he's squeaked through on remnants of his last ace, thinks better of reminding George about settlement referencing that $200.00. "Could have used it to catch up on the grub bill. Probably would have covered lots of fresh-sliced yellow cheese," he laments. "However, better to let the sleeping dog lie," he admits.

The clacking of freshly shod horses on the rocky Middle Fork trail resounds like music. In the waning light of sundown, settling in for a long night under the stars, he mumbles softly to High Ball. "Hold steady, old Pard."

Chapter 5, Thunder in Lightning Creek

Well, Bill, Charlie and I made camp about 10:30 PM, pulling into Saloon Park with 26 head: 23 packstock plus our saddle horses. The trip was uneventful, save for a few wraparounds, a couple of slipped packs and a slow pace on account of the stock being soft. We had taken it easy and rested them on the switchbacks. All told, for a first trip we made decent time with none the worse for wear and tear by the hour we pulled into camp.

There was no moon, with the timbered ridges and higher country poorly lit. At camp, the only set-up wall tent was that of the seventy-year-old cook, Frank, rumored a retired Mafiosi hit man from 1930's New York City. As we began disconnecting the strings and separately tying up the stock, he got up and came out to greet us.

"Whot da hell!  Got a late start didja? ... where's da rest a dem hooligans? ... I tot Tom wuz bringin' da whole hunt in here dis time!"

"Naw, Tom's late, but we waited 'til noon, then hit the trail. He'll be along."

"All four dem hunters show?"

"Yep."

In an hour, we had the string unpacked, turned out to graze and the saddles and gear stacked. We put the saddle horses on picket, down by the creek in one of the timbered meadows where it would be possible to keep an eye on them. Frank hollered at us to come and get the stew he had held.

"So's did Tom have twubble wit dem hunters?"

"Threatened to start last night, but he'll make out ... always does."

"Well, when do ya tink dey show?"

"Well," Bill answered, "I'd guess they're a good five or six hours behind us, and with those hunters being heavy duty and packin' a load, they'll travel slower. Might could show along about daybreak."

By then, Frank's wheels were starting to turn, and with beads of sweat starting to form at the hairline of his wrinkled-up old brow, he came undone.

"Good God.  Dos joiks.  Never dey tink about da goddamned

cook. How da hell does a plan ever turn out!?"

"Alright, " Bill replied with a hint of empathy, "we better throw down this stew and put up a couple of tents, at least fer them hunters."

"Yeah," muttered Charlie, " ... and the cots, as well, or, dammit, Tom is going to be paying the price all the way back to Salmon when the Davy Crocketts mutiny on us!"

"Right, but let's just git 'em staked and tied in, then we'll finish up tomorrow. I'm fer gettin' some shut-eye."

"Roger that!"

"Hey, Cookie, have them elk been buglin' any?"

"I should say ... yessiday morning was colder ... der were tree, mebbe four bulls sounding off up on dat ridge to the west, not mor'n a mile or two off."

"We didn't hear too many on the way in, but she's warming up some."

"Yeah, dey shut up tonight ... only a few sour notes."

"Well, ok, Frank. Thanks fer the feed. See you tomorrow."

"You bet boys."

So, Tom and the four Davy Crocketts pulled into camp just about the time old Bill figured ... near daybreak. They weren't talkin' much, that was plain, but nevertheless we all got up to lend a hand, while Frank fired up the cook stove for some hotcakes and eggs.

We got the hunters off their horses, or, shall we say, "poured them out of the saddle," and sent them to the cook tent to socialize with Frank. In the meantime, we unpacked the two head, unsaddled and fed up half a sack of cubes.

In spite of the obvious fatigue, Tom was grinning.

"Well, boys, one way to break these city slickers of all their blather is to start early with lots of excitement ... scare the livin' crap out of 'em ... then ease up. Long hours, survival and relief spell peace and quiet."

"And that's why you came to Idaho in the first place," muttered Charlie, pulling off the ten-gallon and wiping the brow sweat with a sleeve.

"Yep."

It turned out that the hunters decided to rest their first day in camp, so they caught up on sleep and groceries, driving Frank to distraction over unending requests for cookies, coffee, pies, cakes and a wide variety of snacks. By evening, he was prodding us to get these Daniel Boones the hell out of camp and up the mountain.

In light of pending developments, late in the afternoon, Tom called an old-fashioned pow wow of guides and hunters:

Jack and George were still stoved up from the long ride coming in, so they'd be hunting on foot, in pursuit of that close bunch Frank had heard sounding off two nights prior. Tom wanted to show me some of the higher country right off the bat, so the plan was for the two of us to guide Don and Sam. Before daybreak, we'd head for Bruin Creek and check out the ridges and parks for a big old six-point and satellites Tom remembered had given them all the slip from last fall. We'd wrangle just before dusk, pulling in just enough picket stock for Don, Sam, Tom and me.

Early next morning proved itself, once again, clear and colder, the sharp breeze and ice in the water buckets sending a dose of the shivers as we tanked up, cubed and saddled the riding stock. In short order, Frank called for breakfast, and soon everyone was seated. With several bulls obviously sparring and sounding off in relative proximity, and the two lame, now feeling much more spry, and chomping at the bit, Bill and Charlie were clearly anxious to get rolling.

But Frank, in a frenzy to serve breakfast and simultaneously assemble the sack lunches, was by then vehemently cursing the unsliced blocked cheese for the sandwiches that were supposed to accompany the works. About that time, a couple of bull elk started really going at it, bugling profusely and raking the timber. One sounded way raucous, barely able to reach the high notes, but clearly an old-timer. This got Charlie, Bill, Jack and George fully adrenalized, and all of them started in on Frank to hurry up with the lunches.

Tom could see that Frank was rapidly getting agitated, and in light of former productions, which that character had been capable of, intervention became a priority.

"Gimme that hunk of damn cheese!"

Out came the "Arkansas toothpick," and Tom went to work on the cheese. But Tom is not known for finesse in delicate matters, and before long there was a throwed-down brick and a few jagged, haphazard slices plastered to the walls of the kitchen. With the gunners at the end of their ropes, impatiently standing on one foot and then the other, Jack finally proclaimed that they came on this adventure not to invent the finer points of culinary science, but to pursue and hopefully harvest some bull elk. With several now bugling a near continuum and in proximity, Tom finally declared an end to the cheese venture and stomped off to the horses ... .

In the meantime, Bill and Charlie, in company of their gunners, proceed to move cross country up the west ridge to pull a sneak on the prospective quary.

About then, I drop in on Don and Sam, making last-minute checks on pertinent gear at their tent. Looking over Don's rifle, they come to the realization that he's missing the shells. Must'a got throwed out when the packstock insurrected.

"Well, no problem, Don, take my 30-30."

"With no scope!" He stares with consternation. "Don't know if I can shoot iron sights."

"Take it or leave it."

Ok, so we get horseback and follow Tom up the trail. Evidently he's taken a shining to High Ball, or the other way around, mounted up with no rodeo.

In the dim rays of early morning, one of us jokes about trying out some of the new packstock on the hunters, but this time it all lands on dull ears. We ride for an hour, and by early dim light, have reached the rim overlooking Bruin Creek Basin. We tie up the horses in the timber, off the skyline, and Tom leads us over to a crow's nest rock outcropping that offers concealment.

As the light improves, the terrain begins to offer a series of intermittent tall-grass parks amid the primary canyon below. The remainder is rock slides and dark timber. There is also a minor fork to our left, feeding the main stream from the northwest. Tom calls it the West Fork.

Out come the binoculars and we begin glassing the meadows and snow slides of Bruin Creek. Several hanging glaciers are resplendent as the starting rays light them up amid an ambience of orange and gold. Waterfalls in triplicate lend a characteristic rush to the rimrocked upper basin. It is apparent that man pursues the wapiti as much for the enticement of visiting the splendor of his haunts.

With the coming of light, we note a group of six head over a half-mile off and below us, showing at the edge of a lower meadow:

cows, calves and a spike. Not exactly what we're looking for. In the distance, they appear almost like ants, tan in color, with the tell-tale yellow patch on the back end.

Minutes later, we hear the utterance, a low, ragged growl, ascending incrementally in pitch to enraged squeal, then suddenly dropping off to intermittent groans. It is primeval, ritualistic of the paleolithic sublime. In this place, one forgets the passage of time and links with the eternal.

In short order, the first blow is answered by another, below us, at the head of the basin, then by two more in succession, originating from the West Fork. Soon, we are at the morning symphony, with five or six offering their virtuosi talents. Yet, still we have not heard from the conductor.

All the while, Tom seems to be biding his time, evidently letting the situation develop before playing the hand. There is a hunch that the apparent inaction serves the notion of discernment ... relative to existence and, indeed, proximity of the Maestro.

So, with all the sounding off, the two gunners are clearly getting antsy, and Sam whispers, "Tom, we better get after 'em 'afore they get in the timber!"

"Yep."

A few minutes later, Don is at it. "Tom, that one bull is just below us. Think we ought to get after him?"

"Yep, in a minute."

About this time, another cuts loose, a hellacious, raucous one, clearly a quarter-mile behind us, to the southeast.

Tom lights up like Vegas on a Friday night, looking over his shoulder, neck and back hairs standing. Suddenly he mutters, "Er, back in a minute," as he crouch-sneaks from our perch back over the ridge to the south. In ten minutes, he's returned, the crafty expression and shifty eyes belying, I have a hunch, nebulous intentions.

"Two bulls, satellites, on the saddle between Lightning and West Fork ... . One might go six, but small. The big one's further down, timbered in West Basin about halfway, I'd guess, on the big slide, far side."

"Did you get sight of him?" I asked.

"Well, no, but he bugled twice."

"We never heard him."

"Happens in the mountains ... probably the wind."

"Sure."

"What say you take Don and Sam, drop down and hunt the timber below where that bull bugled in upper Bruin, then head for the forks? Take the West Fork, follow the game trails upstream on the far side. Git where you got some shooting lanes. I'll back track to the saddle and follow the wind downcountry into the West Fork toward the slide and your positions. Might could jump that old bull and send him down them game trails your way."

"Might work. What do you say, boys?" I ask.

"Sounds alright," Sam says.

"But wasn't that snarly oldest one back behind us?" Don hesitated, staring off in the direction of the most vociferous assertion.

"Naw," Tom drawled, "just an old, over-the-hill bull, prob'ly antlers going south, by now, anyway. That type just hole up in the dark, dog-hair timber, loners you can't git at, no way."

"When do you want to link up?"

"Wal, no tellin' ... . Hard to say when and where in all this timber. What say we meet in camp?"

"Alright," I reply, tentatively.

So, Don, Sam and I bail off the ridge and sneak down through deadfall-laden timber into the head of Bruin Creek. There's elk sign in abundance, but the bull that sounded half an hour earlier has shut up, likely deciding to not play his hand any further. Time for Texas Hold'em, I guess.

"Hey John," Sam whispers, "why don't you blow a few notes on that bugle?"

"Probably as good a time as any," I answer, reaching into a vest pocket. Missing! ... as in gone! "Scheisse!"

"Hell's bells!" I hiss. "Damn thing probably fell out on the ride in."

I could see Don giving Sam that sarcastic look, like "Damn outfitter hooks us up with a greenhorn guide who's never been in hunting country, and forgets to bring the bugle ... probably doesn't even know how to blow one!"

It is clear what's coming, so I shut up. Enough sarcasm and blindside, set-up inferences for one day. We proceed to hunt carefully, leap-frogging a few paces at a time, proceeding downstream along several game trails, heading generally for the forks.

A few cows and calves show, making tracks for the heavy timber, but no bulls materialize. In short order, we run out of game trails and are in the worst of thick lodgepole and no quiet. Sam and Don are complaining about having to fight all the blowdowns and muttering about guides who don't know how to get around in the country.

I'm about to tell them to shut the hell up when we hear the shot, and then a second, obviously hitting home.

"Didn't know there were any hunters in this country," I mumble.

"Well, Mr. Guide, there's a lot you don't know, but guess where that one came from," mutters Sam.

"No mistakin' that one!" growls Don.

"Yeah, from just about where Mr. Outfitter has holed up for the day!"

"Yeah, he's got us on a goose chase into the dog-hair timber while he's shooting our big, wall-hanger six-point out from under us!"

"Hm, bet that sonofabitch had no intention at all of ever reaching the saddle."

"Yep, that plan he ran by of coming down the West Fork was just a total crock!"

I'm fed up with all the insightful drivel from these jackasses and tell them to cut the blather. Small wonder the elk are heading for dark timber. We find a way through this jungle and progress toward the West Fork. Eventually, we come upon a pair of game trails that traverse a few intermittent slides, so we move slowly, perusing the clearings. The elk have been using the area, feeding on the riparian grasses and bedding amid the recesses of dark timber. Several bulls have been wallowing near the springs, and the strong odors are unmistakeable. We move at a snail's pace, now, watching for the slightest movement, aberrant shape or off-color entity, while minimizing our presence.

In spite of the grumblings of these two, the surroundings constitute paradise. There is occasional bugling, generally distant. About midmorning, we reach the forks, and with a slight breeze still going downcountry, pause for a smoke break. Sam and Don are beat, physically, and the elk are, by now, well timbered, so we decide to noon up for a couple hours.

By early afternoon, I'm getting antsy, so initially decide to climb the ridge and get a look into the West Fork. With temperatures generally dropping, it is feasible that the elk might be out feeding in this no-moon time of September. So, sure enough, it's possible to locate the big slide Tom was talking about on the far side, and there are cows out feeding. Two, possibly three, bulls are back in the timber, bugling their heads off. Should Tom show in that basin, it is imperative that we get positioned, post haste, on the connecting game trails below that slide!

I return to the two whiners, bitching about where their malingering guide might have gotten off to. "Time for action, boys: There's thirty head a mile off up on the big slide."

We check rifles and ammo, then cross the West Fork and hook in left on several sets of game trails. In a half-hour we're crawling on hands and knees, through alders, fixing to get pinned down by the ever-vigilant elders. There are several raghorn bulls bugling off the trail extensions, and an occasional response coming in above us from an old-timer.

Time for action, so Don stays put in ambush position, while know-it-all Sam follows up to the next tier of trails. We circle back into the direction-changing wind to make a play on the old-timer, who now sounds off in triplicate at one-minute intervals. Time for intervention in the form of an old, expended 30-30 casing, pulled from a shirt pocket. A couple tones will have to do, given the limitations of "high tech."

Now we are hearing the bull thrashing around, raking his horns on brush and alders. Time to pick up a shattered spruce limb and start raking back, punctuating with occasional notes from the casing. Minutes pass, and the bull is silent, clearly trying to pick up our scent by inversely circling the wind. Preempting the efficacy of this maneuver, I signal Sam to follow, making silent tracks downwind. Sure enough. The bull shows amid the fringes of timber, downcountry, at eighty yards, quartering into the breeze, and looking right at us.

We hit the deck.

"Five point."

"How large?"

"Massive."

Sam fires, and down goes the bull; we walk down the incline.

Sam is shaking like a windblown leaf. "My God. I had no idea they were so huge!"

"A thousand pounds, no doubt ... and big as a horse."

The bull is somewhat wedged between two lodgepoles, so we work like demons possessed to extricate, then lay him out for a better look and field dressing. "My God, John, did you ever see antlers like these? They're awesome! Those sabres must be 20 inches!"

"A few, but this five is better than most of the six by's I've seen. Congratulations."

Minutes later, Sam is taking a breather, reclining against a nearby blowdown, when Don shows up. He's in awe of the huge bull. Tells us that minutes before Sam fired, he could have dropped a four-point, broadside, amid a lane in the timber at about sixty yards, but passed. Then Sam shot, after which about twenty cows, calves and two more raghorns paraded by where the four-point had been. It had constituted a spectacular show, that which he had come for, all the way from south Atlanta.

After a few accolades and pictures, I proceed to gut and cape the bull, get him quartered, then head back for the saddle horses. Sam and Don will build a fire, and hole up until I return, anticipated about dark. We'll pack the bull back to camp, using the riding saddles early in the AM.

Well, I get back with the horses an hour after dark, guided by a rip-roarin' bonfire and a sky full of stars. The coyotes are howling up a storm, no doubt on account of blood scent from the elk.

The Davy Crocketts have cut green alder branches to skewer backstrap and fry us up some steaks. Between those and what remains of the sack lunches, we come out alright. No complaints, this time, about any lack of cheese in the sandwiches. Momentarily, I wonder what happened to the Texas barbecue sauce they were supposed to bring. So, the conversation is brief and in subdued tones, and all drift off to sleep, leaning close to the fire, or against supporting lodgepoles. It proves itself a sublime indulgence, amid the coyotes howling, intermittent spectral-colored meteors transversing the hemisphere and bulls bugling from far-off parks. Not much it takes for the supremacy of bliss.

Well, ok, we proceed at early dawn to tend the stock, grab some quick-livered breakfast and pack Sam's bull. The horses offer a bit of protest, but given yesterday's exertions, that proves itself diminutive and short lived. In relatively short order, we have the jerry-rigged packstock in tow and are about to depart the locale, when danged but who shows dragging two saw-bucked empty pack mules, but Tom, riding his favorite, "High Ball."

"Well, I'll be damned!"

We're all shaking our heads in disbelief when the grinning, squint-eyed, old Tom declares, "I'd like to meet the sonofabitch who invented campfires ... mebbe even hone in on the patents, as well."

"So you spotted our smoke?" I responded.

"Yep, and figured you musta had some luck .... Hell almighty, that's one helluva bull! Antlers nearly reach the ground!"

"You git waylayed, Tom?"

"Yep .... We'll talk later ... now let's git the bull repacked on these mules ... and then everyone can ride. We'll go out the West Fork, trails are pretty good ... get to the saddle and go on down to camp."

The ride upcountry proves as straightforward on relatively definitive game trails, as the previous day's jaunt through fallen timber and alders had been verifiably difficult. We pass through intermittent groves of golden-turning aspen, fed by an abundance of riparian springs sustaining the freshness of the pervading grasses. It inspires that the terraced, rimrocked paradise, framed by cascading waterfalls, sustaining glaciers and towering peaks, projects a classic haunt of the wapiti supreme that might well originate from the limits of human imagination. Here, personified, we live the decades of that invention, as though commencing the fruition of God's gift. Could it constitute any wonder that the monarchs had made it home?

So, we pull into camp late in the afternoon, a bit tired and famished, but absent the usual complaining. Clearly, Tom is living a euphoria, and Sam and Don are most certainly close behind. Frank is the only one in camp, and so he comes out to greet us. He bellers that there is ready-made stew and trimmings in the cook tent, and for everyone to help themselves. Sam and Don make tracks in that direction, while Tom and I head for the meat rack to unload the bull, then take care of the stock.

The remainder are still out hunting, having departed horseback in the early AM for Rampart Basin. Frank tells us that George had had no luck the previous morning, and that Jack had passed on a five-point bull at 150 yards late in the afternoon. They had returned to camp, making a plan for proceeding to the upper slides of Rampart Creek in the morning, followed by a foray through some of the lower benches late in the day. In all likelihood, they would be late getting back, so Frank intended to hold supper for all four.

Approaching the meat rack, I am awestruck. Through the bow-covered line of sight materializes the finest set of elk antlers I have ever seen, possessing great width in terms of spread, long and substantially heavy, black tines, polished and ivory tipped. There are six points to a side and strong parity. The massive quarters are noticeably stressing their sector of the cross pole.

Incredulous, I start to question Tom relative to origin, but he abruptly cuts me off, stating, "Let's git Sam's bull hung."

We proceed without incident, yet it is impossible to take eyes off those antlers. They haunt me to this day.

Well, Don, Sam and I turn in shortly after supper, but Tom and Frank wait up for the returnees from the Rampart expedition. It turns out that Bill and Jack saw elk, but couldn't get in on any bulls. Charlie put George onto another five-point at about 200 yards, but the bull got into the timber before the gunner could get it together.

Next morning, Don wants to sleep in, thus to recover more fully from the first two days hunting. At Tom's suggestion, I plan an evening perusal of the low ridges and parks east of camp, an easy walk to a region that has historically been productive.

But with return of all to camp and the issues of the monster six-point becoming common knowledge, most start talking. It begins in whispers, graduates to the undisguised and proceeds to levels of the nearly pervasive and obsessive. Conjecture generates multiple issues, some founded, some not.

Sam: "I told you he holed up back behind us so he could nail that bull."

Don: "Yeah, he came down the West Fork, alright, but for us a day late and a dollar short!"

Jack: "Just a minute, you two. Sam, you took that five-pointer, and Don passed on another. You both had opportunity and cannot say you've been denied what you came for."

George: "Yeah, but Don by rights should have that big six-pointer! Tom shot the SOB out from under both of them."

Bill: "I wasn't there, but with the abundance of game in this country, anyone in reasonable shape ought to go home with one. Seems to me, everyone wins at this game."

Charlie: "It's Tom's outfit. He can do whatever he wants."

Frank: "In New Yoik the Dons were rut'less. They lit'rally got away wit' moider bucuz' dey owned da law. Tom's da law up here, and dis is Rome, Idaho," he tells them ... .

Next evening, after the fourth day of hunting, several of the clients raised the issue with Tom.

He just grinned, raising an eyebrow on the right side, his ten-gallon canted. "Well Slick," he drawled, staring directly at the intimidated George, "the elk god is smiling on this camp, and we got four more days to prove ourselves. It's cowboy up, gents!"

Finally Don, incensed, demanded an explanation, but got nothing more than a grin. "Cowboy up, pardner!"

Next day, Don was still under the weather, so I offered to make a meat run. Tom declined, noting it was holding cold enough, and he needed help in the wrangling department. That evening, Charlie took George horseback, again into Rampart, and an hour before dark they spotted a good bull and eight cows on one of the upper slides. In half an hour, they were on them, and in the fading light, Charlie located the six-point at an edge of uphill timber, setting George up with a solid rest for shooting. When George finally let drive with the magnum, down went one of the cows standing next to the bull.

"Got him!" exclaimed George.

"What the hell!? ... no you didn't! ... you killed a goddamned cow!"

"No!"

Well, the old bull pulled back into the timber, packed up the rest of his cows and headed for parts unknown. Hunter and guide could hear them crashing timber for five solid minutes as they headed for the next county.

"Damn!"

In the fading light, they headed up the slide and found the cow, shot dead center. Apparently George had mistaken some of the abundant deadfall timber for antlers and lined up on the wrong elk.

In a sultry frame of mind, Charlie quartered the cow, and he and George packed the meat on the saddle horses, leading them back to camp. By that time, they were not talking, and after that Charlie, the grudge-holder, had few words for anyone. The expression belied an intent to get even, however ... .

It was just before dark on the sixth day of hunting when Bill and Jack connected on a heavy-bodied four-point on one of the ridges west of camp. George still had an unfilled deer license, and by then, reticent to continue hunting with Charlie, had, earlier that afternoon, asked to go along. Jack had no problem with it, but Bill was reluctant, inclined to avoid further issues over George's inattentions possibly interfering with success. Finally, he agreed, so long as Charlie came with, and guided George separately.

By this time, Charlie had saddled two more head, one a glass-eyed old gelding named Dodge. "The blind riding the blind," he muttered under his breath.

Bill, exiting the corral gate, leading his own mount and one for Jack, had raised an eyebrow, then shrugged his shoulders and tied his pair up at one of the hitchrails. Waiting on Jack, he lit a cigarette, reclining against the corral post. Jack and Tom were conversing in the cook tent with Frank, as he handed out a few evening snacks for the trail. Within a few minutes, the three showed, Tom and Frank joking about the cheese episode of the first morning in camp.

Upon arrival at the corrals and hitching rails, Tom diverted his attention to the two guides.

"Well, you all about ready to head out?"

"Wait'n on those gunners," Bill replied.

Then, Tom perused the saddle horses, checking them out. Seeing Dodge, he stopped abruptly, eyes narrowing.

"You riding Dodge, Charlie?"

"Naw, that's blind ass George's saddle. ... pretty good match, don't ya think!"

"Alright Charlie, yesterday's joke is over! Let's go take a walk. Bill, you and Jack, you all go ahead, and good luck!"

"Ok, Boss!"

Clearly relieved to be away from trouble and encumberance, Bill untied the two mounts, got Jack horseback, and the pair was up the trail.

No one ever learned precise details of the conversation between Boss and guide, as Charlie never subsequently talked about them. In the clear and away from camp, Frank claimed to have been privy to parts of the episode. It became evident, however, that there was a helluva blistering argument, with Tom and Charlie nearly coming to blows over the issue of putting a green client on a night-blind horse on an evening hunt. Yet, by the end of that short conversation, it was clear that future games of Russian Roulette would constitute grounds for a one-way foot rendition of the Bataan Death march seventy miles back to the town of North Fork.

Anyway, by the time Bill and his gunner headed up the trail, Jack was, by this point, admittedly wearing pretty thin, and so had lowered his sights relative to the original goal of a six-point. This, of course, he communicated to Bill, and so, needless to say, both were elated upon connecting with the bull, taken with one clean shot, as the sun's rays faded. Around ten o'clock, he and Bill, both smiling over their hard-fought success, brought in the quarters and rack.

Next morning, Don threw in the towel. He was clearly in over his head, physically, and the altitude continued to bother him, as well. Several of us, including Frank, tried to convince him otherwise, but to no avail. A suggestion of talking with Tom about staying longer was flatly rejected.

At breakfast, Jack advised Tom that the group wanted to pack out a day early.

"Well, ok, but you sonsofbitches are all interfering with a perfect success ratio! It's time to cowboy up! ... hell, I'll take him out myself, and in one long day we'll be at 100 percent!"

"Guaranteed?" George queried sarcastically.

"You up fer a wager, pardner?"

"So, you going to shoot another one out from under your own client, this time?" Sam fired back.

"We'll see! Don, boots and saddles ... ten minutes! Frank, throw together some lunches, would you?"

"Cummin' roight up, Boss!"

"And bring the two best ... High Ball ... and Comanche for Don."

Well, Bill and I grabbed the two head, and in just under eight minutes, had them saddled and rigged, complete with sack lunches in the saddlebags.

By this time, Don, evidently feeling the unwanted scrutiny, wobbled from his tent, Jack's scoped rifle in hand, loaded for bear. He secured the weapon, climbed aboard and followed an incensed Tom up the trail. Catching up, he asked Tom where they were headed.

"Lightning Creek."

At the edge of perception, I heard from the area of the hitch-rails, several of the Davy Crocketts muttering to the effects that although they were neither in awe of the impulsive nor the unconventional, most assuredly there was no envy concerning the recipient relative to excesses inevitably looming amid the forthcoming.

By late in the afternoon, we were all in the cook tent, badgering Frank and awaiting the return. Some were making bets on the outcome along with offering conjecture relative to all the potential what ifs? Amazing, regarding the extent of contrived self-pity over the pretext of ramifications. Victimization prophecy at its cultural worst, I guess.

They came in late that night, riding the saddle horses, Don fading and about to fall out of the saddle. Seeing that, Sam hollered triumphantly, "So, no luck, huh, gents?"

In the lantern light, I could see Tom grinning, expounding that smirk of contempt for the ultimate self-evident ignorance. He climbed down, tying High Ball to the facing hitchrail. There was blood on his hands, yet he said nothing, walking over to Don, now dismounted and assisted by Charlie.

"Good job, Pard!" he stated matter-of-factly, but with a hint of respect, then walked away.

"John and Bill, grab two head of packstock and a fresh saddle horse. Can you have them ready in half an hour?"

"Sure Boss."

By that time, the Davy Crocketts were all standing around Don, while Charlie led Comanche and High Ball off to water and feed. Soon everyone was talking all at once, querying the obvious. Don was at the limit of endurance, so he required help navigating to the cook tent where Frank filled him full of coffee and hard-core stew.

In a short while, he began to revive somewhat and relate the epic venture to Lightning Basin. It was another classic run into unbelievably rough country, full of blowdowns, sliderock and steep terrain, yet at creek's riparian origins, clearly abundant with game. He told of sightings of blackbear, a sow grizzly with two cubs at eighty yards and too close for comfort, countless bald and golden eagles, redtail and goshawks. Toward evening, with the long shadows coming, the bulls had begun the ritual.

The two were more than ten hard miles riding from camp, and it was sobering, the awareness that all of the same would inevitably transpire in the black of night. Don was cognizant of the fact that he would be at wit's end trying even to find a way out of that maze in broad daylight, let alone under impending conditions. In whispers, Tom related that the drainage only got hunted maybe once every three or four years. In spite of the incredible sights, Don was resentful of his state of dependency, yet grateful for Tom's innocuous and disguised concern.

Nevertheless, they rode down into the drainage to the extent that it was possible to navigate, without killing the horses, then tied them up short to a pair of saplings and proceeded carefully on foot, mindful of placement and relative to the obvious. By the witching hour, they were leeward to a long riparian slide, shaded amid foliage and long grasses, and virtually hemmed in on three sides by ten to twelve bulls, the majority of them signaling fight. The concerto increased in intensity and volume, achieving maxed crescendo, and approached continuum, the vibrations apparently tremoring the ground, itself. The rattling, crashing of timber and brush, tossed about by massive antlers and crushed under thousand-pounder weights, resounded like incoming, danger-close barrages resembling nefarious accounts of Verdun and the Western Front. Seemingly, there would be no all-quiet this time.

In fading, ambient light, filtering amid tall spruce, half a dozen appeared sequentially over several minutes, filing in tiers along peripherally arranged, horizontal game trails.

In silence, Don incrementally bolted the round, while Tom braced the rifle stock with his jacket. They continued waiting, Don sustaining the scope on the heavily antlered six-point, but, at Tom's insistence, perusing for one larger should such entity appear before light completely faded. Finally, with Don's expressed attenuating ability to discern the cross hairs, Tom gave the nod, and in a flash of reverberating, rolling thunder, the great six-point, shot through

64

the heart, fell stone dead in his tracks.

"Never even flinched," Tom asserted. "That's how it's done."

...

Midnight, back in the cook tent:

Don claims it is one of the greatest events of his life, the remaining bulls so unaccustomed to hunting pressure and presence of man, that they held in proximity, as though undisturbed in the wild, while Tom field dressed the six-point. Don says such events link contemporary man with the Paleolithics and our origins, and that he would cherish the sublimity of that once-in-a-lifetime connection with man's primeval echoes, for the rest of his life.

The ride back to camp, under bright stars, darkness and Universe seemed profoundly different, this time. They stopped once to roll a smoke. When Tom lit up, the glint in his eyes said it all.

## Author's Note

Years later, on a cold winter day, I looked up Tom, within the town of Challis, still abiding in the same old diminutive trailer he had lived in for twenty years, the living quarters adorned by a small television and a very large set of elk antlers. Besides Tom, those cigarettes and a bag of chew, there was no room for much of anything else.

Living the dream and another day in paradise. Semper talis!

# Chapter 6, Lard and Fishermen

The summer following the fall season I worked for Tom Schmittmann, he came up short on pack trips. A friend of his, we'll call him Joe Thompson, had a ranch out of Challis and outfitted summer and fall seasons adjacent in the same mountain range, the Yellowjackets. By this time, Bill and Charlie were working for the Panther Creek outfit through August, promising to hire on with Tom, again, for the fall. So, wanting to keep the old crew intact, Tom colluded with his friend, Joe, to hire first Frank and later me for the summer. The timing worked out fine, so everyone agreed and got on the same page.

The initial group of clients turned out to constitute eight fishermen from the Atlanta region, and they showed up as scheduled the tenth of July, for a ten-day trip. Most had been out with Joe, the previous summer, on an outing of similar nature; thus, given that they had the general routine under their belts, no one anticipated any surprises.

They had encountered excellent fishing that past summer, with golden trout abundant in some of the high-mountain lakes. The outing had gone off well, with most commenting about the spectacular scenery and splendid grub thrown together by the cook. Yet, it was perceived, and no doubt correctly so, by Joe, that a primary impetus for the return business was the splendid fishing.

Well, old Joe turned out to be quite an intriguing character, as well. Tom used to talk about him some, mentioning a few of the quirks of the old-timer ... . Said he was a helluva hand with a rope, and used to insist on the hired men following suit, thus for getting the stock caught prior to boots and saddles. Tom also mentioned that old Joe could cut corners and find stray aces better than just about anyone else he knew. Evidently, he could make "green" out of coyote bait.

I asked Tom how it was that he possessed such insights, and what kind of "green" was he talking about? Tom replied that once he worked for the old piker, but the only elaboration came in the form of a sly grin and the usual squint-eyed look.

So, prior to showing at Joe's place, I spent a few weeks trying to figure out the two ends of an old lariat, then in early July and a few days before the trip was scheduled, drove up to the ranch.

First to show was Stan, a tall, lanky kid, about twenty, who wrangled and packed for the outfit. He had worked a couple years for Joe and the old man, Jake, evidently Joe's father, and claimed that he was the only hand who had survived the ordeal of employment. Claimed the others had bailed at one time or another, but that when he tried, the old geezer had threatened him to the point that sustainable occupation was the only viable option. Stan said that now he couldn't quit, even if he wanted to. Evidently, there was one payday with this outfit, at the end of the season, and if you didn't make it, there would be no remuneration.

"So, where're Joe and Jake, and is Frank here yet?" I asked.

"They're in town ... went to Salmon to pick up groceries and last-minute stuff for the trip. They'll no doubt stop off at the Cowboy for a tall one on the return. Frank and Jake go way back, so they'll be up half the night getting caught up."

"Alright. I'd like to take a look at the horses. Wonder if you might offer a tour."

"Sure, why not. We've got part of the bunch corralled out back. Most of them will be on the trip ... . Follow me."

Well, I got the tour, alright. Right through a minefield semi-junk yard full of barbed wire, concrete, rebar and every imagineable automotive assembly known to mankind, and probably going back to the '30's ... .

Finally, we got to the corrals, a cobbled-together excuse of baler-twined and wired rails and posts holding about twenty head of parrot-mouthed, u-necked old-timers. Most looked about 100 pounds off their feed, and upon mention of the fact, Stan replied that Joe never believed in wasting funds on putting flesh on horses throughout the winters.

"So after hunting season he generally turns them out on short feed and cheap sagebrush, bringing them in for a few days before the start of summer season and pouring the feed to them. Always seemed to work out in the past ... and any surviving the blizzards and coyotes were probably tough enough to get to camp and all that 'free' mountain grass, anyway."

Jake had owned the business for thirty years since the war, before recently selling half-interest to Joe, and evidently claimed all along that it wasn't a bad way to operate most of the time.

"Hm ... ."

67

Speechless, I wondered what Tom had up his sleeve in this deal, but resolved, however, not to make any rash judgments, pro or con, until there was a chance to speak, face to face, with Joe and with Jake.

Well, the three finally showed back at the ranch about 2:30 in the morning, and all were packin' a pretty hefty load. Stan pointed out that Joe was driving, or you might say making an effort to steer the pickup, a rough-running 1940's half-ton, seemingly getting by on one lung. Evidently, he had to prematurely cut the power to the rig, then let it backfire a couple times and glide to a predetermined halt in the driveway to the front of the listing-to-the-side ranch house.

So, we proceeded somewhat with the necessity of introductions, while Frank and I exchanged salutations. Notably, Joe and Jake were both thin faced and dark eyed. If Joe could pass for mid-sixties, then bald-headed Jake had to have reached the early eighties. It was noticeable that Joe possessed a long, bony, hawk nose that bent to the right, and that Jake's inclined far to the left. That raised the question as to whether the same south paw had connected with both, but at different venues and disparate angles. Neither had a great deal to say, but Jake told Stan to show me the bunkhouse and the outhouse, not necessarily in that order. I was hopeful that the two were not one and the same. Upon execution of that directive, I noted several holes in the roof of the former, but fortunately none was in alignment with the relevant bunk. Clearly, the outhouse had seen better days, but living in paradise, who the hell needs one, anyway.

Next morning and breakin' daylight, Joe gave us a holler, and we walked over to a set of corrals different from the one Stan had shown. On the way over, Joe said he had heard from several sources that I could get around these critters when it came to nailing on shoes. Well, that raised an eyebrow, as the thought occurred as to what might be coming ... . Yep, when we got to the initial corral, there stood eight of the snarliest-looking, raw-boned, snake-eyed democrats I had ever seen. Most looked like they'd just take delight in kicking somebody's head plumb off, and wasn't it simply a pure coincidence that, sure enough, they were all barefoot?! So, guess what? Joe needed 'em all shod, and yesterday.

About that time, I started to inquire about pay, but Diamond

Joe suddenly got real busy rounding up shoes, nails, anvil and tools from the nearby tack shed. By the time Stan managed to get all of it brought over, Joe had departed on an "emergency" run to town, to pick up last-minute items, forgotten yesterday, for the trip.

Well, this sorry bunch of mules had its kickers, alright, but I'd never encountered so many damn biters. Always it's possible to deal with those "light foots" on the rear end by tying them up, but that doesn't preempt those blindsides originating from the opposite end, while working on the fronts.

So, Stan and I went to work on several, agreeing to gang up on the hard cases. Well, the first was a hard case, alright. That "jackass" played like he was going to let drive with a rear, thus hammering Stan while working on a front. However, this turned out to be just a feint; the real blindside got accomplished by reaching around and biting Stan in his own rear. Now when a horse or mule bites, it seems as though he's got to complete the entire cyclical process, and he cannot back off halfway through the endeavor. So, if he connects with the bull's-eye he's painted on somebody's back end, he's going to shred some flesh ... and that bull's-eye turned up on the back of Stan's brand-new pair of denims. Dropping the front, Stan cut loose with a blood-curdling howl, yowling bloody murder, at that damn mule named Chester. There would be gunsmoke, alright, and it was certainly time to gang up! We tied up a hind, threw that character and hog tied him. Then one of us sat on his head while the other got him shod. You can bet that when we let that sonofabitch get up, we got the hell out of the way. Most all of the rest were trouble one way or the other, all three- and four-year-olds Jake had picked up, for a steal, at a recent horse sale in Idaho Falls. Some bargain!

Well, we got 'em done; took all day, with gimpy old Jake hobbling over, from time to time, from the house to see how we were coming. The more bruises and hard knocks we took from those heathens, the longer Jake would hang around telling stories about bygone days when they made real hands instead of boy scouts. Finally, around 2:00 in the afternoon, we had had just about two bellyfuls of Jake, so one of us asked when the hell this cub scout outfit might roust out hungover Frank long enough to throw together some breakfast. Jake muttered something under his breath about the cost of damned pogeybait hotcakes and taters, then gimped off back to the house. It wasn't long before Frank bellered, "Come git it, or it goes in the fire!"

...

At "breakfast," Jake hinted that the mules would be my responsibility for the summer pack trips. Hearing Stan sigh with relief, silently I wondered how the hell it was going to be possible to get all of them packed on any one particular day, let alone make any time on the trails with this renegade bunch. Any thought of having to run this string after dark, as often occurs in these scenarios, was simply overwhelming. Rather suddenly, the realization came home that it would become imperative to make friends with all eight, or face the hard-and-fast consequences of unforgiving insurrection every step of the way. It was fixin' to be one helluva long, hot summer.

Next day, the Atlanta group flew into Salmon, and I met them the following morning after Joe brought everyone up to the Middle Fork trailhead. They brought every imagineable kind of gear, lots of rattling fishing poles, tackle boxes and other time-bomb stuff which most certainly the mule train would accommodate with great enthusiasm. The saving grace was that the mountain of excess duffel and equipment was compensated for by a rather paltry supply of grub.

Stan had heard Joe talking with Frank about the issue, with Joe insisting that there was no need to load up much in the way of groceries, on account of "all the fish everyone was going to catch." It had been that way last summer, and the one before, and nearly always those dudes had just wanted to eat fish! Might just as well save on the green backs for a rainy day.

Well, we got all packed up, and it was time to really screw those packs down tight. There was Frank's kitchen, a little grub, a couple of wall tents, white gas, camp accessories and a whole lot of duffel. The diamond hitches were pulling those heathen mules nearly in two.

The plan was for Joe, Frank and Stan to lead off with the clients, heading for the Kitchen Lakes and camp, while the eight mules and supply train pulled up the rear. That way, if the new bunch started the Third World War, the guests would be ahead and out of the line of fire ... .

It does not take long for WWIII to get off to a glorious beginning. About an hour up the trail, just when it seems as though those critters are starting to get the hang of things and properly line out, there is one helluva commotion. Looking back, I see the pack on #3 slamming into a "too close to the trail tree," and the damn thing starts rattling away. In short order, half the string is bucking like hell, and several are launching those packs clear into the lodgepoles. Hell almighty, that third pack is the culprit. It won't shut up! After a while, things settle down tenuously, so it's time to bail off Stranger and go back. Losin' pack on Jiggs, so time to pull the latigos and dump the whole mess. Still rattlin' and Jiggs will have no part of this, so takes off up the slide and wedges among more of the string. About time to toss that damn pack, but better to discard that notion and pry open the contents, instead. Evidently, the large green duffel bag labeled Atlanta is the culprit. Yep ... some jackass packed his alarm clock, and it's set for 10:30! An hour later, most of the train wreck is baler-twined and duct taped together, hitches are rethrown and we're up the trail. Mules and greenhorn packer, alike, are getting one helluva swell education, and future adventures as well as the Russian Revolution are on the horizon.

Next episode is mule #7, Lester, getting bit by #8, Pancho. About the third time this occurs, it's time to stop the whole works, tie up Stranger and go back there. Lester wants to kick the irritation, so he lets fly at me for causing it. The boot goes in his belly a couple times, and the pair get switched around. From the tail end of the string, Lester won't be kicking anybody. Getting back to Stranger, next order is to untie, mount up and jerk the whole bunch up the trail. Next perusal to the rear reveals Lester biting the hell out of Pancho, timing the venture so he won't get caught in the act. In response, Pancho fires bass ackwards with both feet.

Time to go back and separate them completely. When I start to slide by, #5, Chester, the first renegade we shod two days prior, lets fly and scores a broadside, recoiling off a knee. Time to pull him out of the string, lead the culprit some distance away and lay into his behind with a stout limb. About the time he acts as though inclined to fire back, he gets stared down and dared to try it. This cools him down, so I grab Lester and bring him to the head, thus honoring him with the status of lead mule. We're back in business, at least until next time. "Clickety-clack," we're up the rocky trail.

Twenty minutes later, we're into a swarm of bald-faced hor-

71

nets, and are they on the warpath! Evidently, Joe, Stan and the dude string must have gone through and stirred them up. Well, Lester, then Luke, Ginger and Jiggs managed to stir them even worse. About 200 descended and bombadiered Corky, Stonewall and those behind. Thus, packs, pots, fry pans, groceries, bedrolls, duffel, fishing poles and cooking utensils are scattered from hell to breakfast. This greenhorn packer is cussing a blue streak, and it's not helping one iota. Never could believe how a convention of democrats in crisis could invariably create more chaos out of order! For a while, under the circumstances, not a helluva lot could get done in the restoration department ... .

Finally, it was apparent that the baldfaces were growing tired of their "fun," and retired to parts unknown. Time to begin the chore of catching up the membership, tying them to available trees, blow-downs and anything else that might serve as tieable to, thus restoring some order to the convention. The exercise came down to baler-twining shredded latigos back together, duct taping sawbucks and pecking around like a witless chicken trying to pick up all the useful and utilitarian debris. After considerable deliberation, the greenhorn came to mule #6. Black Kettle, as in war chief. He'd managed to bash his load of wooden boxes full of groceries into several trees, thus splintering the panniers and scattering the vittels. There was" blood" all over the landscape and remnants of the pack cover. However, much to relief, this turned out to constitute false alarm, as the salient issue boiled down to several broken half-gallon bottles of ketchup.

Now about that time, who would come up the trail but Ranger Rick, our local friendly and helpful custodian of the forest, who knowledgeably informs all as to civil laws and penalties relative to littering public lands. Greenhorn packer was in no mood to be sociable, so about all that came in response was a disgusted, incredulous glare, and back to work. Well, next the helpful guardian-of-the-wild, encountering the abundance of "blood" on tall timber and equipment, came unhinged and demanded an explanation. The reply was that this was the treatment the last bureaucrat who came through, got, not thirty minutes prior! Abruptly, Rick removed his hat, spasmodically crossed himself, ran a hand through his sweaty mop, fumbled the unused ticket book back into a shirt pocket, and, ashen faced, departed into fading sunlight.

Two hours later, and cobbled together, we were back in business. I was cursing Diamond Joe, old Jake and Tom Schmittmann with every imagineable line of cowboy-blathered vengeance, perpetrators of those manipulated deals!

Now, apparently, those democrats were either tiring or getting that trail stuff figured out. There hadn't been an insurrection for several hours, other than a few unintentional wraparounds accompanied by commensurate-knowledge bumps provided by Mother Nature, herself, on those brain boxes. It seemed as though the switching-around exercises succeeded in separating the grudge-holders.

Then just before dark, that damn rattling pack on Jiggs started in again. Off Stranger and back there before the train wreck had a chance to get launched. "Woah, boys ... easy now ... it's alright. Easy!" Reticent, but not eager for another disaster, that train of mules held firm, snorting a bit, but allowing the packer to proceed with the rope jerking. Off came the pack, then the duffel and damned if there wasn't a second alarm clock, this time a real McCoy, Big Ben bonger! It was set for 8:00 PM. This greenhorn was ready to throw the contraption off the nearest cliff into the worst of nasty sliderock, but reconsidered. One more day in paradise.

Well, the mule-kicked left knee had swollen profusely, making it difficult to get off and on, as in horseback. There were hopes that Wishbone Frank could apply a home remedy once everyone was settled. That was, if ever!

To get the mind off trivia, Jiggs fully obliged, an hour later, with another rattling pack. By flashlight, amid profuse snorting and tail-swishing mules, off came the duffel, and the source was once again revealed. This one, set for 9:00, caught a high-trajectory hurl off the tall mountainside, accompanied by lyrics of *Tick Tock, Yer to the Rock,* in harmony with the sounds of latent mass destruction.

Well, even the extra-sociable democrats finally got enough on their insatiable palates to call it a night. In spite of laying rather poor odds on ever getting this paltry menagerie to camp, danged if along about midnight, Stan didn't come riding down the trail ... to lend a hand and to remind yours truly, "never been in the country," about the cutoff trail into Kitchen Creek. That accomplished, we pulled into destination somewhere around the hoot-owl hour. It was good to have some help, given the tank being about empty and the knee turning balky. By the time we got unpacked, unsaddled and all put away, Frank had us a warmed-up supper. I hobbled to the cook shack, and, in delerium, thought it was utopia.

There is vague recollection of telling Stan, Frank and a few of the others, the previous day's adventures, but all of those good things finally had to come to an end. So, time to hunt up the bed roll and a good tree, and it was off to see the wizard.

No idea when the witching hour came, but what seemed like a brief nap ended abruptly with Joe apologetically bringing to roost an apparent crisis. Evidently, one of the guests, a feller named Keith, was missing his alarm clock, and had also left his sleeping bag in Atlanta. Joe was just wondering if any extra bedrolls had gotten packed, and if I knew anything about the clock. Well, I paused, feigning "wake up syndrome," then after a bit told Joe about the "bloody" pack covers from Black Kettle, and that fatso Keith should consult with Jiggs reference the alarm. Perhaps they could all work something out. It was clear that fat Keith must have been so adrenalized over the fishing, that he had no intention of sleeping, anyway. Hence, all the clocks and no bedroll. Of all possible explanations, that one made the most sense.

Back to sleep, and there was no stirring until midmorning, long after the fishermen, Joe and Stan had left camp, departing on foot for the lakes.

Long about 5:00 PM, Frank got busy in the kitchen, firing up the stove, greasing a couple of fry pans and, clanging around, had camp chairs and tables arranged for a big fish fry. He said Joe told him to get ready to put on one heckuva feast with all the trimmings, spices, biscuits and salad made, for the first anniversary of last year's "Golden Troutslayer Jubilee." Unbeknownst to yours truly, yesterday's packer had no idea that the panniers on Lester held some eight gallons of "Old Rotgut," brought all the way from the Deep South, for the occasion. Hell almighty, that might have come in handy the night before, but no dice! Beginner's luck, I guess, so they'd have to do for tonight's community effort. In the meantime, it was occasion to fumble around camp and become useful, so Frank organized a firewood-cutting and water-hauling detail.

Well, 'long about 7:30, Frank's got everything ready, but no fishermen, Joe or Stan, yet. We're thinkin' they must have hit one

74

helluva school of those 16" goldens up there, and had forgotten all about the socialist endeavor in camp. Frank was getting downright crotchety over their being an hour and a half, and counting, late, and "why da hell nobody ever tinks about da goddamned cook!" Finally, I've had enough of the wood supply and hen-pecking Frank, so time to head out in the direction they all departed, this morning.

An hour up the old trail and a couple of lakes, and still no south-of-the-Mason Dixon anglers. Shadows were getting longer, so I was trying to figure out from the tracks, what the hell. "Musta tried these close ones, first, but then headed for greener pastures." Was about to head up into one of those higher benches likely housing more lakes, when there was a clear shout. Whole group was coming down the trail from off the ridge. I hollered back, and Joe answered. Lending scrutiny to the entourage, it was not looking like those creels were full of two-pound lunkers.

Well, the closer they got, the more down-in-the-mouth all were looking, and those creels were plumb empty! The eight were all complaining, "no fish and out of cookies, candy and granola bars." Nobody had caught a damn thing, and in fact, nobody had even seen a fish. Joe was fit to be tied. "It's the same lakes we fished last summer, this time ... a year ago."

Stan confirmed, "Same dates, last July."

I made some joke about "the monster grizzly that musta showed up in June and ate all the fish," but no one laughed.

We got to camp just about sundown. Frank was in a helluva mood over "everyone late," but laid off after hearing about the fishing. In short order, supper was on, with Frank unceremoniously divying up the lettuce, spice and biscuits, to be augmented by an abundant second installment of ditch water.

After a second long day at altitude, the expectant, famished guests were leering with consternation at the lettuce and biscuits. One of them asked Frank which the hell entre the spices were to go on ... the lettuce or the hardtack? At that point, Frank was at the threshold of losing it, so he walked out of the tent and stomped off, while Joe broke out a bottle of the Rotgut. Well, it did not take long or rocket science to figure out what effect high altitude and eighty proof might have on a bunch of tired, half-starved, fat guys from Atlanta. I've forgotten exactly, over forty years past, but it seems that after indulging three or four half-gallons of the stuff, the trout-slayer jubilee rapidly degenerated into the human-slayer disaster.

As I hunted up the bedroll and proceeded to cut some z's, Joe could be heard rather loudly claiming that he had a hunch there was better fishing in the as-yet-untried lakes to the northeast of camp. In the meantime, it was going to be the job of the packer to resupply the camp with beefsteak and taters. Joe, in spite of the influential Wellers, did not hesitate to roust this unlucky soul and, for the second time in 24 hours, inform the greenhorn of yet another addition to the job description. Proferring a profound level of gratitude concerning that update, I rolled over and caught a few more hours of sleep.

Nevertheless, Stan, Joe and I were up before daylight, wrangling in the packstock for the long ride out. With two of us saddling up, Joe was on the shortwave to Jake, informing the old snake of our dilemma. With everyone in camp glued to the conversation, Jake promised to bring a "whole freezer" of elk steak and other vittels to the trailhead, and would have it, with a string of fresh packstock, on the spot when I got there.

Frank had got breakfast, basically lettuce and one biscuit with spices, ready, and handed me a sack lunch for the saddlebag. You guessed it, more of the same. It was time to tell him that he might want to save the lettuce and spices for the starving clients, so I crammed the crumbling biscuit into a shirt pocket and handed a scowling Frank the sack back.

Stan later related that the empty pack train got out of camp about an hour after daybreak, along with the good fortune of missing out on all the bitching and moaning that inevitably developed. Those green mules turned out pretty docile, that day, owing, one can be sure, to the high altitude and strung-out blues from ordeals on the way in. They seemed a bit off their feed, so owing to regrets, it made sense to take the time to water them at all the major creek crossings. They actually travelled rather well, with only a couple of wraparounds and no kicking. Seemed like in spite of the swelled-up knee, we all got along rather well and made the trailhead by dark. There was optimism that through all that ordeal, might arise a modicum of trust.

Well, time to unpack, unsaddle, feed and water. Unfortunately, the only things missing were dinner and Jake. At issue was famished-to-the-point-of-chewing-on-the-corral rails. Frank's bis-

76

cuit lasted 'til noon ... guess the error was not to have held onto the lettuce.

Time to drive to North Fork, call Jake and find out what the hell. Might not hurt to get some supper, as well. That foray produced no answer at Jake's, and the restaurant was closed. So, it became imperative to call the Cowboy, and damned if Jake didn't come to the phone! By that time, the tank was about empty, and so was the level of patience. Jake was slurring the words, and it was hard to make any sense out of excuses. Time to tell him to meet at the trailhead at 9:00 AM and hang up. Next agenda was to drive to Salmon and get a room at the Shady, supper, shower, sleep and breakfast. Adios Jake, Joe, bitchin' fishermen and kicking, biting mules. Tomorrow will come soon enough.

Arrival at the trailhead, 9:00 AM. Feeling much better with the tank half filled, but no Jake. He showed at 10:30, driving, one-handed, the old truck, and pulling on a pint of Old Raven with the other. It proved interesting, spotting the rig a mile off, weaving up the county road, spewing gravel and dust. He missed the turnoff into the facility, screeched to a halt, backed up and pulled in.

The old man jumped out, slammed the door and offered the bottle, which got politely refused. Then from the rear of the pickup, he went to throwing ten to twelve boxes of formerly frozen packages over to the corner of the corral. Time to lend a hand by proceeding to organize and balance the loads.

Well, any rocket scientist can count loads, boxes and folks. Dividing the former by the latter results in an estimated fifty pounds of steak, burger or what the hell for each dude and hand in camp. About the time the head-scratching began in earnest, Jake interrupted and stated that he had a helluva deal goin' in Salmon that could not wait. "Got to get back to the office!" So, I waved ga'bye as Jake took off back to Salmon. "Hope ya make it alright, Pard."

Well, no fresh string of packstock. Guess Jake musta sold 'em in exchange for more paltry booze and road kill. Anyways, by noon it was boots and saddles, and clickety-clack, we were off to see the wizard. No trouble with those demos, that time. Guess the hype of the convention was over, and we were back to the doldrums.

It was pushing the ninety-degree range, guessing, of course, and two hours up the trail, it became noticeable that those packs were starting to look a little strange. Another two hours, and the sack panniers were seeping grease, or something, so it was hold up fer a look-see. Yep, it was grease, alright. Not sure it was going to make sense indulging in steak dinner when we made camp ... could be old Jake was just trying to cut corners by making substitutions, as in road kill. Anyway, this greenhorn wasn't totally born yesterday, having gotten a pretty good sack lunch thrown together in Salmon, that morning. In a pinch, it might just have to last awhile, as in several days.

Well, it was fixin' to be another long one ... although the string was clacking along quite well. ETA was looking like about 1:00 AM. As the sun went down and the stars began to show, entertainment amid the tall and the uncut came in the form of a few of those meteor showers. As the sky grew darker, the phenomena grew in frequency. Some of those streakers covered much of the hemisphere, nearly spanning the horizons, and offering the myriad of spectral colors, with burnouts coming after several full seconds. It was pleasant and blissful to forget all the excuses and whiners for a while.

The bliss lasted only a few hours, for when we pulled into camp, it was 1:30 in the morning, all the lanterns were lit and everyone was starving wide awake.

So, they all proceeded to mob the hitchrails and corral area, asking all sorts of questions, precariously loaded with accusations, liabilities and charges. "Why are you late? Where the hell was Jake? Did you have more trouble on the way in? Why didn't somebody send food in on a helicopter? Did you really bring in beefsteak, or is it just horsemeat?" The packer was speechless and too tired to concentrate on any answers. Finally, the response was to ask which question they all wanted answered first.

Finally Joe intervened, stating, "Let's get to unpacking these critters so Frank can get started."

In the meantime, Stan related in private that, over the past two days of absence, the group caught a grand total of two fish, both of them pitiful looking, dilapidated, raw-boned suckers. After much badgering, Frank finally gave in and fried them up, ceremoniously dividing them into eight portions. Apparently, the most recent excuse of supper consisted of the remnants of wilted lettuce, one powdered excuse of a biscuit and a rat-boned smidgen of sucker filet. Stan further related that the entire camp was by then on the verge of mutiny. Yet, Joe Diamond had managed to resurrect the situation by expounding upon the "outrageous" speculation that the Game Department might be the cause. That succeeded in raising a few eyebrows. Joe recalled reading, last spring, in the local papers about some project by which several of the Middle Fork high lakes were going to be stocked with golden trout, this summer. The others were simultaneously supposed to be poisoned to eliminate undesireable species and restored later. He thought maybe someone in the department might have gotten the wires crossed and given the order to poison the wrong lakes!? I recall hoping that the trend might not continue by which the same "enlightened" would proceed with closure by restocking those "golden" purged lakes with more suckers.

Everyone had been anticipating this event for the past several days, and all those pie-eyed, ganted-up, old fishermen stared in eager expectation of the forthcoming feast of steak and taters. Frank leered like a jaundiced scarecrow, a pair of butcher knives at the ready, while Joe, his bony hawk nose canted even more to the right, displayed a pained, unhopeful glare that even more might go south.

Ok, so we got to unpacking and subsequently dragging the first meat panniers up to the cook shack where Frank, by then, waited with several chopping blocks at the ready. He then, cutting tools in both hands, with dexterity tied into the first packages. A few well-placed, precision slices and gashes, and ... "Wot da hell!?"

As the freezer paper got unravelled, all of us gaping, anticipatory birds came unglued, like squawking crows staring in consternation at the unpalatable result. Suddenly, one of the Georgia bunch blurts, "How in hell do they expect us to eat this?!" Then another, "This is nothin' but garbage!"

Then Joe grabbed another package and started slashing with greater intensity, producing the same result. Stan and I then went to work on a second set of panniers, with no improvement in the findings. It was not long before the court convened and passed judgment upon the perpetrator. The verdict was "pack us the hell out of here, now, ... and we'll deal with you, Mr. Shyster, when we get to town and our lawyers!"

Well, I was too tired to participate, plus Stan and Frank had listened to three days of constant bitching, so we all went hunting for our bedrolls and some peace and quiet.

Thus, Joe was left to persuade the clients to spend the night reclining and to wait for daylight. In the meantime, Stan and Frank were detained and had to dig a deep hole in which to throw six hundred pounds of lard, to keep the foul mess inaccessible to bears. Amid their labors and cussing, I heard Frank grumble that that damn Jake, in his besotted stupor, must have gotten into the wrong freezer at the ranch house.

Long about 3:00 AM, those two finished the funeral and burial detail and finally settled into peaceful bliss and a few z's. This was short lived, however, as several of the Georgia birds came squawking out of their moth-eaten tent, evidently mortified by a large, marauding, black bandit of the furry variety, which, enroute to the recently found winter hibernation cache, had converted the canvas residence into a wind tunnel. The furry fiend, however, had paid not one iota of attention to the mortified humans, but, rather, had made tracks straight to the burial site and was proceeding to exhume and devour the contents. After some minutes of chaotic digging, thrashing around and clawing away, the sundry contents, paper and grease were scattered from hell to breakfast. Finally, Frank got up, located the sawed-off double-barrel in the cook tent and filled the back end of the intruder full of double ot. The old bar left a bawlin', crashing brush, timber and blowdowns ... heading for parts unknown. Dammit, if that didn't take the cake ... our ready-made bear stew, pourin' coal to the fire and haulin' ass!

Of course, by then the Georgia boys were all awake, agitated, and it was "United we stand!" Even jaw-waggin' Joe Diamond could not talk reason to them concerning their resolve to vacate this "hell on earth!" Finally, Stan and I got saddled up and were off to horse wrangler's paradise. We got the stock located and brought them in about daylight ... none too soon, for the duffels were weighed, balanced and ready to throw on our freight train. No alarm clocks, this time! ... and no bees, hornets, rattlers or any other trouble, save for endless bickering, whining and threats of retribution all along the going-out trail. From the sounds, it was clear that they were intent on contacting every lawyer and better business bureau north of the Mason Dixon and west of the Mississippi. They were going to hunt down that scoundrel, Jake, and drown that besotted sonofabitch in the Salmon River. There were few goodbyes and fewer tips at the trailhead.

All the lip service came to nothing. In those days, there were neither victims nor entitlements ... just mostly winners ... and only a few losers.

As previously related, back in the late seventies, I purchased a hunting camp in the Thorofare of Wyoming. This comprises a wilderness region near the south and east Yellowstone borders, and the locale offers major concentrations of seasonally migrating, as well as indigenous, elk. The organization used to access the country by way of trailheads out of Jackson and Cody, and so we initially ran four or five pack trips for fishermen and tourists in the summers, plus several fall outings to hunt elk, deer and moose.

Of course, any guide who manages to, at some point, purchase an operation, finds himself compelled as first order of business to learn literally every detail of the territory, the drainages, secret passages and game trails. Naturally, that includes the primary and secondary locations where the elk are habitually feeding, watering, where they are taking refuge when pressured, the bull wallows, preferred fighting grounds and lots more. Circumstantially, anyone awake through this assimilation process concludes the obvious; that to learn all is unachievable, but to learn substantially is sincerely ambitious, and so the process must be ongoing and ultimately a lifelong commitment.

So, after a couple of seasons into the process, it was slowly becoming evident that a threshold approached by which there were fewer surprises. Intuition seemed to be replacing the pedantic processes of detailed analysis. We were starting to achieve acceptable levels of success in terms of filling our clients with mature bull elk. Occasionally, benevolence and luck conspired with perseverence to gain the rewards of a few notable trophy-class results.

About the third fall season into the operation, I was guiding a former client of the previous outfitter. This hunter named Bob was a most agreeable character, and had booked the previous winter, a referral by the predecessor. We hit it off immediately.

It was September, a favorite time in the wilderness, owing to the symphonic atmosphere brought about by bull-elk rituals of bugling, fighting and collecting harems. One afternoon, we decided to proceed with a foray into Ross Creek basin, a drainage only a couple miles distant from camp. The drainage was particularly heavily timbered, yet had a prominent slide about halfway up on its south side.

Incipient upon entrance to the mouth of the canyon, was a faded horse trail of sorts, and this was subsequently enjoined by tandemly arranged game trails which, although disjoint, in a general direction led on up to the slide.

We planned on tying our mounts in proximity to where the horse trail petered out, and subsequently following the game trail network on foot, methodically hunting our way up to the clearing. With the coming of late afternoon shadows, we plotted our arrival for when those old bulls might well be tuning up.

...

Recollection is that this was at about the two-thirds mark of the month, and that particular year there had been a hard freeze a day or two prior. This had proven to constitute the catalyst that really set the rut into motion. The bulls were going at it, fighting early and bugling well before darkness, herding the cows and combating each other most of the night. Nearly anything would set them off, including coyotes howling -- even blowing a few pathetic notes on an empty shell casing or just plain forceful whistling in imitation of the initial tones.

Well, upon approach into proximity of the slide, we really went on point. Remaining within the shadowed timber, both of us concentrated on glassing carefully between the spaces, in hopes of sighting horizonal geometry, off color and of interest, that might become visible. Bob seemed particularly intrigued by an abundance of sign and concomitant heavy use of the game trails which were in proximity, and pointed out several sets of substantial bull tracks. Delighted, I was not surprised in the subsequent minutes to pick up several melodic vociferations, emanations seemingly originating from proximate timber which circumvented the far edge of the slide.

One particular series of harmonics really gave a case of the grips. It is in some ways difficult to describe, but the best assessment is that we both agreed the origination constituted a series of five full ascending tones. Now the majority of elk hunters are aware that most bulls produce three, perhaps four tones, climbing the octaves as the rage increases. With attenuation generally come a few raucous grunts, grumblings, etc. This particular one, however, offered less rage, rather beautiful lyrics, no grunts, and esoteric attenuation, falling away to the lower, or sixth, termination pitch.

At the time, such resonance had never been previously witnessed by the writer, nor has it since.

That evening on the Ross Creek slide proved itself memorable beyond expectations. After those initial opening bars, and amid fervent hopes of catching sight of this splendid orator, we crawled on hands and knees through shadows to better seating. Remarkably, the zeal for hunting gave way to ardor for listening and passion for acquiring simply a glimpse.

...

We move deliberately and at separate times, the second motionless and offering hand signals as the first proceeds with caution. Finally, Bob signals that there are cows moving, filtering out of the timber into the tall riparian grasses that arise in proximity to the slide-feeding trickle. Amid the waning rays of golden sunset, we plant ourselves in the shadowed conifers below the slide rising through black timber to the high rims of the canyon. We perceive the sublimity of distant waters, of falls tunneling the high-glaciered rims.

Once again, the great orator effuses his declaration, as though for acoustical emphasis, the lyrics reinforcing as they bounce around the canyon walls. Minutes later, a heavily antlered five-point tests the wind, then shows at the demarcation of timber, midlevel on the slide. Shortly thereafter, he is accosted by a second, accompanied by eight or ten cows, which come in opposite and higher up. The first is now sounding off and tearing up a cluster of saplings above his original position on the clearing, while the latter herds the cows back towards incoming timber, and then stands forward, subsequently starting to walk down the cut. The two now close the gap, pausing momentarily to tear up more saplings and rip at the ground. Turf, grass and down timbered limbs are tossed, thrown around, building frenzy for the forthcoming. In fading light, we observe the shadows squaring off, and hear, subsequently, the crashing of antlers ... .

An hour later, we reached the horses. It was pitch dark, so we tightened cinchas and stowed rifles and gear, using flashlights to attend to details. Giving the horses their heads, we were off to camp, clacking across rapid-flowing Ross Creek.

The galaxy was in full flower, that night, and the coyotes howled forlornly, perhaps in anticipation of the harvest moon which would become prominent in a few weeks. An hour later, we could see the faint lights of camp, starting to show through the gaps in timber. We halted at the hitchrails, just then perceiving the lone, lonesome whistle, the "odd six," in the far distance, signaling yet another oration. In anticipation of reply, we paused for several minutes from the unsaddling, but the only responses were the silence of the forest and a muffled rushing of the far-off stream. Finally, an old hoot owl taunts us with, "Hoot, hoot ... hoot, hoot, hoot ... hoot: try again ... later, see ya ... later."

Over the next weeks, years and seasons, there followed a number of such incidents. Always in September, there were massive tracks, large numbers of cows and odd, six-toned bugling. In October, he seemed to break away from the herds and assume a solitary role ... and so, the legend of Piccolo Pete grew with the times.

One year, two of the guides threw in and devised a plan which they deemed would smoke this cagey monarch out of the recesses of dark timber. To date "Old Pete" had never been sighted by any of us subsequent to his discovery of several seasons past. The full range of evidence constituted what, thus far, has been related, but invariably excluded any visual appearances of the concerned. Some, myself included, in weaker moments began to question the viability of existence, itself.

Kelsey and Slim were each guiding two hunters from the West Coast that trip. It was mid-September, and both had pined away all the past year over attempts, throughout several seasons at this legend, gone south. "Old Pete" was haunting me, as well, so there were no objections upon hearing the two guides, in the late-morning hours after breakfast on the trip's third day, scheming as to just how their joint operation was destined to corner the elusive ghost.

It seemed as though early that morning, Kelsey had taken his two clients horseback and downcountry to peruse the park line, hoping to pull an old-timer out of the lair by bugling. Just breaking daylight, they topped out on a timbered ridge overlooking one of the basins, tied the horses and descended on foot. As the rays began to turn the rims to copper and gold, Kelsey set up his pair of gunners amid a series of outcroppings from which they could sustain visibility relative to a series of meadows located across the canyon and several hundred yards distant. He then approached solo, pulling amid dense timber in proximity to the parks. Raising the bugle, he offered a blast, which was momentarily answered by a bull evidently skulking along the edge of one of the meadows. A continuation of the verbal sparring produced enhanced participation by several more of the animals, and before long it became clear to the hunters that their guide had led them to Nirvana. By the time Kelsey returned to them, both were on point, clearly excited about the prospects concerning an evening battle plan for action and adventure.

However, with the amber rays starting to blend the timber, and with the bulls winding down a bit, it was the next series of audibles which got the attention of the guide. These originated from a point somewhat beyond the meadows, aforementioned. Distinctly they comprised five incrementally ascending tones, one attenuating and refined, with a decided absence of subsequent grunts, and with this perception, Kelsey brightened. He pronounced that the oration had originated from "Old Pete," perhaps the greatest bull in the Thorofare.

And so it was that morning that Kelsey, Slim and their four gunners began their quest in earnest to corner "Old Pete," and settle the score.

The plot came down to Kelsey returning to the morning's posting with his two clients setting up in the same manner, overlooking a pair of the distant meadows. Slim would proceed to a point well beyond the meadows, which, in a general sense, correlated obliquely with the incoming wind direction. His direction of travel would align obtusely with the subsequent route of travel of Kelsey's group, which would latently fan out and carefully approach the clearings. They would move silently as possible, but in spreading scent, this would tend to drive any timbered and actively feeding elk in the general direction of Slim's pair. Given the extent of Slim's anticipated placement of his gunners, it was hoped that the drive would affect not only the elk grouping, relative to the previous morning, in vicinity of the meadows, but "Old Pete" at some point, as well.

Further, Slim's pair of hunters would be setting up on a fairly extensive slide, full of tall grasses and fed abundantly by game trails connecting from the meadows. With the two gunners well concealed at disparate elevations, and with an expected crosswind prevalent, relatively viable directional perception could be achieved over most of the arterially oriented incoming trails. The plan, although not foolproof, offered fair percentage chances for success among the participants.

Well, any elk hunter knows that those basin winds can get tricky. Generally they tend to, by midday, move up the canyons. Often and early, they'll cease and desist, with a slight flow seeking lower elevations. This reverses shortly after sunrise, with the air becoming less dense, of course. An inverse occurs late in the day, when the energies lower, and entropy collapses. Nevertheless, the entire trend patterns go south owing to the vagaries of Mother Nature, quite prominent contributions arising from sudden orthogonal crosswinds and reversals, to some known as blindsides. Owing to unpredictability, these can neither be planned for nor anticipated, rather, only reacted to. So, at times we all find ourselves frustrated, possibly buying ourselves a few minutes in delaying ultimate compromise of the best-laid plans, circling back into an aberrant wind, or, at worst, having to reassess and proceed with reinvention.

Well, the plan went into motion when all left camp, horseback, about 3 PM. Kelsey and his two gunners set up in the timber short of the meadows and waited a full hour for Slim and party to get fully situated at their end. The shadows were prominent when they spread laterally and began their drive. Within twenty minutes, they had a mature six-point on the ground, quite possibly one among the crowd encountered early the same morning. After field dressing the animal and covering it with pine bows, Kelsey led the group laterally along the canyon. Crossing the meadows, peripherally, it was within a short time that they began to encounter large numbers of cows and calves. There were chances at a younger four-point bull, but Kelsey's second hunter had eyes for better antlers. So, all proceeded cautiously, much of the time pinned down by thirty or more perusing cows.

By about an hour prior to sunset, Kelsey and his gunners had worked their way virtually into the center of the herd, and were literally surrounded by the critters. The bull scent was extremely pungent, with the guide on point, looking for the antlers of the century. However, in short order, the slight breeze began to get chaotic, and subsequently swirling badly, sending the by-then-on-point elk in various radiating directions, concentric to the gunners. Clearly vacating the country, at least one substantial group headed off in the anticipated direction of Slim and company.

At that point, intent on a last-ditch effort to catch sight of the ultimate quary, Kelsey, hoping for a shot, proceeded to maneuver his remaining unfilled gunner to the nearest clearing. No such luck. Consequently, with the majority of the herd on the move, the group proceeded in the general direction of Slim, but with fading hopes for the elk reversing their direction of travel.

Slim and company, of course picked up on the shooting when Kelsey's group connected on the six-point. That put them all on alert, and from their posts and optimal shooting lanes, they kept an intense vigil.

It remained quiet, however, until about an hour before dark, the only activity coming from chattering squirrels and some raucous whiskey jacks and camp robbers squabbling over a coveted stash of pine nuts ... . But then the branches began to break and rocks to clatter, and there were incoming hoof sounds, cows barking amid the far-zone game trails feeding the slide. The turmoil was of such magnitude that Slim found no necessity of giving a heads-up to his clients.

In short minutes, the elk began to show, ghostlike images amid the timber, chaotically filtering into the slide, instinctively pausing to lend momentary scrutiny to surroundings, then accelerating to the near side, abruptly catching the human scent, recoiling and scattering, then fading ... and they were ... gone. A pair of mature bulls showed, but no cigar ... and no Pete. In fact, no bugling, and within short minutes ... not a sound.

But he was there, somewhere. Next morning, Kelsey and Slim left camp, heading back to pack in the six-point bull. Horseback, they decided to check out yesterday's situation in some detail, so they pulled on over to where the elk scent was strongest. It was not long before they picked up, amid the marshlike wallow, the set of huge tracks, clearly those of a dominant and remarkable bull.

Of course, without snow, these were at best very difficult to follow amid timber, pine needles, dry ground and sliderock. Nevertheless, following the trail of yesterday's bailing main herd, revealed, in short order, that the protagonist did not remain with them. Within a few hundred yards, the absence of telltale tracks lent credence to the notion that the old-timer had pulled off orthogonally and had, no doubt, beat feet over a  conveniently located  timbered saddle, into the safe haven of Yellowstone Park. That turned out, at least to constitute the consensus of the two guides, who, upon returning to camp, related their verdict. The prognosis for the scenario repeating itself that season was highly unlikely, but the three of us vowed, that should one similar present itself the following September, we would set up, as first priority, guide and wide-awake client to cover "Pete's Saddle."

Well, over the next six years, there were a number of such encounters, and owing to the stories and inevitable bar talk, the legend grew. Always, in early fall, evinced the peculiar six-toned bugling, monstrous tracks, large harems and thirty to forty pairs of protective eyes vigilant for intruders. It seemed that always dark timber was part of the equation, coupled with a proximate escape route or two into Yellowstone.

Throughout the winter months, as I proceeded to book the subsequent two camps, potential clients used to call out of the blue, all hours of the day and some nights, to ask about Piccolo Pete. Some booked years in advance, paying up front and full price for the chance of pursuit or even to hear him sounding off.

Years later, I guided a novice from the East Coast. He was an accomplished academic who taught American Literature at Penn State, but had never hunted anything other than whitetails near home. He had booked the last hunt in September, and so I had the chance to take him out. We rode one of the high ridges which backed off the park line, dismounting and tying up off the skyline to glass one of the basins. Later we set up on a more distant crow's nest overlooking the canyon below. Amid the waning hours of that afternoon, the concertos had been brief and infrequent, but as in nearly all hunting endeavors, the persistent and the optimistic ultimately got the nod.

And so it happened. Far below us, in the fading light of evening, fate smiled amid dark timber, and we heard the six tones, a little strained given six years of history and long winters ... nevertheless unmistakeable. "Old Pete," I mumbled.

Looking over, I could see the light go on in the dusk.

Quietly he unloaded the bolt-action. The voice revealed emotion. "That's why I came," he said. "Just that was enough, getting to hear that one. I won't be hunting anymore, this trip ... just hiking and fishing."

In six years of pursuit, we never sighted Old Pete.

## Chapter 8, You Elephant Stompin' Sonofabitch
## or, The Perfection of Soul

Along about the second fall I worked for Old Fritz, one of the guides and the foreman got into it, and we wound up a hand short. That meant temporary promotion to the status of the vacated. Consequently, in spite of a few objections, the author wound up inexorably linked, for a solid week, to Herbert, an overweight plumber from Kalamazoo. At the time, only minor significance manifested from the zoo portion of the nomenclature and the idiosyncrasies of out-of-state clientele.

Now, in spite of the obesity issue, no one bothered to provide a heads-up relative to the dissonance factor. Apparently, it was obvious to everyone else.

So, the second hunt that year, we all arrived in camp with Steve, Pete and I guiding a group of five hunters. My client, Herbert, had booked with the outfit for, to date, several past seasons, but had yet to connect on an elk. It therefore made some sense to ascertain hints as to pertinent circumstances, by asking a few innocent questions of the contemporaries.

One clue was established early by the fact that Herbert got "housed" in his own private tent, situated quite some distance from the rest of the camp. The first night revealed Fritz's justifiable reasoning: that the reverberations of unmuffled snoring kept many of the personnel wide awake for most of the night, in spite of the extent of quarantine. Subsequent questioning of camp staff revealed that they deemed the concerned, even if bound and gagged, fully capable of inadvertently disrupting even the most intense bars of a Shostokovich concerto, and on a sustainable basis. Further, Pete simply called him the "candy man," but would say no more. Nancy, our cook, merely laughed upon my inquiry as to her impressions, but did finally comment concerning his remarkable nervous habit at meals of scratching all parts of himself on a cyclical and intermittent basis.

Well, first day out hunting, I began to assimilate some of the hard lessons, alluded to by others. Early that morning, we saddled two head, and headed up one of the ridges north of camp. Several bulls were bugling intermittently a couple of miles out. So, Herbert and I tied up, got the wind right and proceeded into timber adjacent the first clearings. Twenty minutes later, with the breeze diminished and constant, it was time to reposition Herbert within a few of the shadows, and wait on our quary, now anticipated upwind and incoming along a prominent game trail.

Well, danged if a half-hour later, here come six head of cows and calves, filtering into the meadow. There was a bull, but hanging out, bugling back in timber and out of sight. Minutes into the process, I was glassing the far edge, burning holes in the dark recesses of timber with ten-power binos, trying to put antlers on something. Herbert, however, seemed to be losing patience, fidgeting around and fumbling with a scratchy, down-filled, nylon vest which infused bedlam as he tried to recline against deadfall. In short order, the cows and calves displayed their contempt by turning their backs and abruptly vacating the premises. This greenhorn could just barely abate venting fury at Herbert, who then wanted to wait around for the bull to show! Well, hell eureka! Why hadn't I thought of that? Or preempted the vest before we left camp? We returned to base, turned the horses loose and jettisoned the vest, making plans for an evening foray downcountry to the double slides.

Hours later, we were on site, shortly before sunset, hunkered down amid the alders and out of vision relative to the quary. There were elk sounds above us, amid the lush riparian grasses fed by the runoff. Judgment suggested a bull, perhaps 300 yards distant and in the dense adjacent timber, likely along an arterial feeding the clearing. The wind was not the greatest, so time to signal Herbert the intention to consider an alternate approach. Actually, there existed also the notion that a little distance might have tended to diminish the earlier racket issue, contemplating that a bit of temporary solo communing with Mother Nature might have produced the desired calming effect. However, such contemplations proved themselves ill founded, as, emanating from several hundred yards distance, came a crackling commotion, subdued sounds of amusement, and oppositely directed, a latent vacating of real estate by yet another herd of spooked elk. Hell almighty! Furious, I stomped back through the alders and down timber, back to my client, who, crunching away, was busy feeding several fat, chattering squirrels from a large bag of crispy potato chips. So much for solo meditation!

By that time, glaring with severity, I was about to come uncorked. Preemption came in the form of that bristly old panda bear, who reached into, that time, his noisy, shiny new, nylon, ripping back pack, throwing in more rattling and crackling for good measure. Crzz ... kkk!

Smiling broadly with palms extended, he innocently extracted, then generously offered, a second noisy bag of the damnable stuff. One was disarmed to the point of acceptance, taking respite on the nearest blowdown snag. What can one offer to blissful existence? Immanuel Kant sought perfection of soul: Guess I must have been in heaven! So we both crackled away until dark, feeding voracious squirrels.

Next morning, the top story was that the afternoon prior, Pete and one of his hunters had encountered a group of elk. They had run into them at the edge of timber off one of the slides downcountry from camp, determining that a heavily antlered five-point bull was in their company. The two had made an epic two-hour stalk, playing the wind and cat-and-mouse with the bunch. Finally, the hunter dropped the bull just at dark. Pete and company would be departing momentarily to pack in the elk.

So, I was really starting to feel the pressure as the lone, solo one-on-one guide, to make something happen. Time to grab the horses.

Herbert showed, amid the rest of the group, at the hitch rails twenty minutes later, eyes bright and smiling. He was anxious to show off a new camera, complete with 600 mm, 6 pound lens, some two feet in length, which he had affixed. The entire apparatus weighed eight or nine pounds and hung from his neck. In addition, there was a sizeable camera case, lens case, another for tools, flashlight complete with lanyard, scissors, binoculars and vise grips, all hanging off of Herbert: Herbert the hunter impersonating Herbert the plumber! All the rest were snickering, and one of the hunters, in a fit of gripping laughter, nearly fell off his horse. Finally, Pete, horseback, proceeding to roll a smoke, asked if I needed any help. "Very funny!"

Well, Herbert's saddle went on "Old Grady," a kind of wild-looking, black-and-white paint with a large circle of black around one eye. I was not liking the look in that eye that was looking over Mr. Herbert. It was about to say, "No dice, Pard! ... time to take a second look-see at that hole card!"

As Mr. Plumber approached to mount up, I had visions of

Herbert, hung by all those crazy slings from the highest tamarack. Being not in the least enthused at the prospects of having to somehow unhang Herbert, I called a halt to the process and proceeded to advise the same as to alternate approaches to the madness. It was a relief when snickering Pete and company wished us the best of luck and finally rode out of camp. Silence ... at last.

Well, ok. We got better organized: rifle in the scabbard, ammo in the saddle bag and Herbert mounted on a negotiably tolerant Grady. Finally, we were up the trail headed for Bruin Basin. An hour later, we tied the horses at the lower end and skulked around for most of the day. Turned out, we weren't the only ones in pursuit. Extraneous rumblings turned out not to constitute a factor, this time, as the drainage proved to be loaded with grizzly tracks, to which Herbert remained oblivious, so dissonance and various timely vociferations, although annoying and ominously habit-forming, proved to offer some preemptive defense relative to chaotic encounters. The elk turned out to be decidedly absent, and so we backed out of there just before dark, grabbed the stock and rode. The horses showed prolific signs of the "look-behinds" all the way back to camp.

A day and a half later, it was drizzling a bit, so we headed out on foot for Swift Creek. In spite of the alders, it was possible to remain quieter, and not long after reaching the approximate midway point of the drainage, we encountered a major game trail complete with fresh elk tracks. There was just a skiff of fresh snow, so that sign looked to be verifiably recent. Must have been about four head, with one bull track which I pointed out to Herbert. We got after them, stalking slowly and keeping tabs on the direction of nearly absent breeze. Over the next hour, several times we caught glimpses of cows, and so it became optimal to motion my client to chamber the round and take the lead.

Well, clickety-clack went the bolt action, and the elk bailed. I glared at Herbert. Flashing a disarming smile, he offered a wrapper-crackling candy bar, which, through clenched teeth, was politely declined.

By the fifth day of hunting, three hunters had filled. I was really facing the pressure. It was time to advise Herbert as to the merits of silence, or at least attempts at quiet.

Early next morning amid recent snowfall, Pete wrangled in

some fresh saddle stock, and so Herbert and I headed northwest from camp toward Falcon Creek. Steve and Pete had spoken highly of the place, offering detailed input as to how the terrain could be approached. There, the high alpine basin at its upper end offered a series of tall slides with plenty of intermittent timbered cover. Riding in the darkness and gaining elevation, paralleling one of the main fork tributaries for twenty minutes, hopes of "time for action" began to pervade what, up to now, had attenuated to an assessment of "no chance," relative to success. Horses were tied as the incipient, early rays tunneled under hanging clouds, turning white mystery into gold clarity.

It was time to put one eye on the first slide and adjacent timber, perusing for our quary, and the other on Mr. Herbert, in case it became necessary for intervention relevant to the bolt action, or one of the other tricks this character was capable of, in regard to pertinent details of nutrition. So far, so good. The elk seemed to be co-operating, as well, as fresh sign was evident, and a bull was bugling down below and laterally left of the slide. Noted was the fact that it would be harder to make racket in soft snow, so there was optimism that things might have been looking up.

Those hopes and dreams were abruptly shattered, however, when the bull's ever-more-proximate bugling was vociferously answered by several bouts of Herbert's abrupt and spasmodic fits of loud coughing and sneezing. Being laser focused on the bull, I was initially seized, then lifted by the cataclysm, temporarily gaining several feet in elevation. Upon returning to ground, I quickly noted the bull breaking cover, gathering his cows and hauling ass to get the hell out of the country. In parting insult, the entire clan made the point of crossing the final slide at full throttle, just out of shooting range and pouring coal to the fires.

By that time, I had truly gained a full belly of this goofball spasmodic excuse of degenerate humanity, and could take no more. It was time to consult with Old Fritz concerning this incorrigible klutz. To add insult to injury, upon our return to camp, we learned that Steve was then the hero, having filled his second hunter with a large black bear. (The client was thrilled, planning to have a rug made for the den in his new house.)

It became, by then, time to inform Fritz that we would be pulling out all the stops and heading for the snarliest, nastiest piece of real estate in the entire hunting country. "That would be Combat Creek." It was loaded with foul dog-hair thick timber, blowdowns thick as fleas, sliderock and abundant grizzlies. I planned on taking "Herbert the Klutz" into that hell hole, and he could damn well make all the racket he wanted to. Logic said that if it was that bad, the elk wouldn't be able to keep quiet, either, so they wouldn't be hearing us any better than we them. That should have levelled the field. Also, I told Fritz that we wouldn't be coming back until we had meat and antlers, or Herbert had run out of potato chips.

So, Fritz and Nancy threw together some huge sack lunches for us, and out of pathetic consideration, packed all in soft, padded plastic bags for reverberation-damage control.

Horseback, we departed camp about 3:00 AM. Pete accompanied, thus to bring the stock back to camp after we topped the divide, north of Falcon. From that point, Herbert and I would drop off into Combat, proceeding to approach prime country from above. And so, just after daybreak, our "grinning" wrangler wished us the best of good luck, departing off the ridge as the two of us began our descent into the forbidden and heavily timbered canyon.

From the top, it became clear that there was one locale from which it would be essential to keep quiet. At the head of the basin, a tall and prominent slide with accompanying lateral timber, might well be holding elk. It seemed unwise to bypass the opportunity, so we held up short and plotted our moves. We reached a rock outcropping adjacent the clearing about halfway down, holding up for appraisal and noting a few cows starting to show amid intermittent springs a few hundred feet below us. Minutes later, through incoming, easterly blown spindrift, more cows and calves came into view, then moved on into adjacent timber. No bulls, however.

But there was one old-timer, carrying on profusely amid the next dark, snowed-in timber, beyond the slide, and it became apparent that he would be worth a try. As the cows cleared, below, we proceeded to cross the slide, working our way into an anticipated parallel orientation, thus keeping the breeze in our favor.

So, it became imperative to quietly exploit the advantage by dropping down on the bull's ongoing assessed location. Quite abruptly, Herbert was instructed as to the critical and meritable essence of quiet, as in silent footsteps. With a breech shell prelocked, loaded and safety engaged, I became the gun bearer, in the lead and prepared to hand Mr. Client the fire stick at the proper moment. I was not about to let Herbert get away with any false moves, and furthermore, all crackling materials, to include candy and gum wrappers, potato chip bags, in fact, paper of any kind, and potential clinking stuff were thereby jettisoned. To Mr. Herbert's dismay and furrowed brow, I put the entire pack of obnoxious party favors behind a large rock.

Herbert showed the consternated, sad-clown face of losing a long, lost friend. There were no condolences. In fact, to this day, over forty years later, there exists still considerable satisfaction over what apparently constituted resolution of the Herbert noise issues, once and for all! I was more than fed up!! It was time to proceed. In sync, and moving precisely, we descended to lower elevation, keeping our eyes peeled for the old-timer.

In twenty minutes of inching away, we reached more level ground, where footing and snow conditions were more conducive to our efforts. We'd dropped a full thousand feet without mishap or spooking the quary. Things were indeed looking up. The bull was still sounding off, and Herbert and rifle were thus far intact. It became evident that the bull was now retrograding, and proceeding into darker timber; we began to enter a stand of monstrous tamaracks and massive blowdowns. Worse, there were those infernal alders, so we had to pay close attention. The old-timer could be only 200 yards distant ... perhaps even less, and it was imagined that I could hear his breathing. We conversed in whispers ... moving singly and in slow motion. First I moved ... then Herbert, center forward, with me watching, willing myself to control the minutiae of each foot placement, toe first, then weight, rolling weight to the ball, then setting the heel ever so precisely. Finally, we had to cross this snow-laden, monstrous blowdown, which I could barely manage, and which exceeded stubby Herbert's stride and spread. It would have to be a Herbert's leg up and over, with the client going first. We were nearly point-blank with Mr. Bull, whose bellering seemed to fill the whole north woods. Well, up and over went Herbert, who, with my help, managed the launch, but fell short in the landing, chaotically hanging up mid-air in a maze of broken limbs and protruding tree roots, finally, over an eternity of perhaps ten seconds, extricating and crashing voluminously, on terra firma amid cavernous alder-like, sundry obstacles, in a cataclysmic heap. And, of course, subsequently followed by a clattering of hooves of a consternated bull vacating the country. Incensed beyond reason, I vaulted the obstacle, landing in the middle of Mr. Herbert, who sat unhurt and bemused.

"You damned elephant stompin' sonofabitch!"

Well, prior to finally doing in my client, several minutes of quiet, cool-down contemplation produced Plan B. It was going to be a major chore even getting Mr. Herbert out of this hell hole, let alone back to camp. Therefore, it would constitute the wisest option to conserve energy and rest Herbert. We were at the periphery of a quite decent slide and piece of hunting country, fully equipped with abundant incoming game trails, so why not let the client hold the fort while the hothead scout proceeded with a foray through this extended jungle, made lots of racket and tried to run something with antlers across the path of the gunner. Detailing all of this to a contrite Herbert, produced immediate agreement. We worked out a time table, and shortly thereafter, I departed for the Combat Creek jungle.

In short order, it became evident that this maze was some Mecca. From the extent of the terrain, blowdowns, foul, heavy timber and intermittent game trails, it became clear that the place was the ultimate elk haven, almost never intruded upon by man. There was abundant feed among much of the dark timber, where concentrations of our quary produced the odor of barnyard manure. Periodically, the vibrations of the animals moving out ahead lent credence to the impossibility of their sustainability of silence while attempting to move in this primeval place. Hours later, amid longer shadows and inspiring light, the imploding return began. Back on track and closing on the point of origin, I heard the shot of ten thousand years. Spellbound, I wondered about the tree that fell in the forest.

With recurrent doubts haunting a jaded consciousness, I made haste. Thirty minutes of jungle-fighting later, and worn to a frazzle, I found Herbert and company at the point of origin.

Well, "and company" comprised a splendid, trophy-class, thousand-pound, six-point bull that would take the honors for the hunt and the season. He was shot dead center, with Herbert, red faced and beaming, gloating in delight over his good fortune. By that time, Mr. Herbert had metamorphosed into Mr. Great White

98

Hunter, at least in my book, and I was ecstatic, yet then feeling guilty for disallowing the camera. Herbert merely smiled, offering some crackling potato chips from yet another noisy bag. What?? Curious, I took a look-see at my client's stakeout, ambush position from which he was supposed to have set up. It was littered with no fewer than forty-three!! ... of the worst variety crackling candy wrappers, compliments of the nylon backpack. His most recent tracks led a full snowed in, one thousand feet back up the mountain to where we had earlier jettisoned all the worthless ballast ... and back!

After the trip had ended, I willingly, in fact voluntarily, accepted demotion and resumed the packing job. Old Fritz used to laugh about it all, figuring I was far more willing to take my chances with the mules and meeting up with "Old Clyde, the Dynamiter," on the Holland Creek trail, than to risk having to guide another Herbert. He was right on that score.

To this day, I think about Herbert every time I see a bag of potato chips, or a chocolate bar, or, for that matter, a can of sassperilly ... and sometimes, contemplation drifts into notions of the perfection of soul.

Mr. Kant, you shoulda met this guy I took elk hunting one time ... .

Back in the old days, that is, goin' on about 1979 or '80, I purchased the South Camp. Along with that outfit came tents, camp equipment and accessories, tools, several vehicles and, above all, ten head of saddle horses. Man, was I proud of them. To this day, I recall every detail about them in living color! They still frequent midnight dreams among all months and all seasons. What a great string that was!

There was Pal, obviously a palomino and a quarter horse. He was literally plastered with brands, on the hips and shoulders, among them several prominent amid the region. He had to have been pushing mid-twenties at the inception of the outfit. Clearly, in his day, he must have been a handful, for no one could have kept him around long enough to establish reliability. Nevertheless, upon our acquaintance, it was clear that he had mellowed considerably, and his steadiness as a dude horse had become well founded. He was also notorious for sustaining an eye-teeth jarring, bone-rattling ride all 32 miles into or out from camp. We were later to find out a bit more, abruptly, under somewhat different circumstances:

Old Pal turned out to be even more talented in the wrangling department. It was during one of those early seasons, 'long about '82 or '83, when we came up short on some of the lease horses in camp. Early on, we were generally short on outfit horses, relative to the fall, as funding limitations curtailed expansion in the materiel department. Consequently, I had to lease the differential between what we possessed and what was necessary for operating.

Now those "borrowed" stock were generally pretty savvy. They had been around the block, so to speak, having been for years contracted for, summer and fall seasons, collectively by most of the outfits amid the peripheral country. Consequently, they had assimilated generally extensive knowledge of large tracts of the region and some knew all the hideouts. They were good manipulators, as well, finding admirably ingenious ways of getting out of work, and with the most "opportunistic" features of timing, conveyed the talents to their contemporaries. One could swear that some of those Mafiosi bunch-quitters had even contrived to learn our work schedules and indelibly commit them to memory.

The Thorofare country is literally covered in abundance

of timbered parks and lush meadows, and by September, the tall grasses are curing out. Horse feed is pervasive, and some of the best fixin's frequent the riparian areas of the abundant drainages. For stock becoming savvy to the art of hiding out and avoiding work, some of those havens back in the recesses of drainages far from camp, literally became Shangri Las. The malingering recluses had found home, and there they would remain until discovered and rooted out.

Hence, what became an outlaw's paradise, turned into a wrangler's worst nightmare ... .

One night, a couple hours prior to normal wakeup, I couldn't sleep. Time to fire up the dining tent stove and warm up the coffee. I was met by Willy who had the same problem: "No horse bells!" Strange, being bone tired, but having to deal with insomnia. Vagaries of the profession, I guess.

So, we saddled up the two picket horses and took off in opposite directions to find the eight missing renegades. Long about midmorning, we were back to camp seeing if Dick might fix us a late breakfast. No horses and no bells. Should have packed a lunch. The quest continued for several more days, but to no avail. The outfit's hunting horses were catching double duty and starting to show resentment. Time to double up on the cubes for them, and find the bunch-quitters. Willy and I were racking our brains, figuring that if we didn't find the horses, soon, the cubes would be gone shortly thereafter.

First day of looking, Willy recalled seeing a few stray horse tracks up Ross Creek, but which seemed to fade out amid the well-travelled game trails. That had been our only clue, thus far, so I decided to saddle up one of the old-timers who knew the country and go have a look-see.

"Grab one of them elders," I said to Willy.

"Any one in particular, Boss?"

"Naw ... Pal, Luke or Muley."

Ok, so time to put Pal in gear for a test drive. Man were those dudes right! He was the worst, bone-jarring, rattling piece of cobbled-together horseflesh imagineable! Even tried him out in second gear ... and it just got worse! Finally, put him into a lope, and much better: smooth as silk! That was the answer, at least in short spurts. Well, ok, so we are headed up the trail along the main fork, then cut left, diverting into the lesser canyon. We stopped often, trying to make out a few jingling horse bells.

You know, those damn bunch-quittin' renegades have been known to hole up in the head of some paradise, hideout, remote canyon, grazing all night, bells aclangin'. Then, 'long about sunup, bloated with all the fixin's, they'll stand absolutely quiet, bells silent in the first rays of sunrise, sight unseen, making sure the wrangler passes unawares. Damned foul heathens!

About the fourth time we stopped, I was concentrating, straining to hear a hint of a jingle bob and watching Pal's radar ears. I was about to start thinking there's some infinitesimal allusion to a far-off, head-of-the-basin clang, yet carried by distant winds from, dammit, no doubt another canyon, when Pal impatiently pulled on the reins. His snort broke my concentration, and suddenly he was pulling on the bit. Well, this old-timer certainly wasn't born yesterday, and his radar was clearly better than mine, so time to give him his head. We were up the next game trail, jumping blowdowns and cracking limbs ... off on the next arterial. Damn, it hurt when the knees caught those burned-out lodgepoles! We'd gone into second gear, and the carcass was arattlin'.

Finally, it was time to rein him in, but he would have no part of it. Any back pressure on those reins, and he was on the fight, snorting like a freight-train steam locomotive! Time to quit the battle and just hang on.

Well, we covered ground in this manner, enduring ten minutes in survival mode, emerging from blowdown timber into a series of parks, connecting riparian meadows which precede the final half-mile to the head of the drainage. By then we were into horse tracks along the creek, and hell almighty they were fresh. Then, unmistakeably, there were horse bells, clangin' away, as in close and voluminous. We climbed up through a timbered slope overlooking the creek onto a benchmark meadow ... and there were the bunch-quitters, the whole fat and sassy tribe of eight head, faces buried amid the tall grasses. We proceeded to get around them, as in circuitous maneuver ... .

Finally, Grady and Elmer snap to that they've been apprehended, and up come those heads out of all that grass ... . Looking bewildered, but not one bit guilty! Now all are apprehensively watching us.

We got in on their blind side, and the basin rang with the war whoops and banzais. Instantly, Pal went to open throttle and pouring on the coal. He wasn't born yesterday, nor the day before, either! Time to hang on or face the Little Big Horn! Quick thanks to the Boss for the invention of bear-trap saddles ... .

Down the canyon, crashing deadfall and timber, it's the wild, Whoop Up Trail, horses bucking, kicking, biting, jammed up in the blowdowns. Finally manage to get Pal to let up on the pedal against metal ... . Main trail though, we're geared up and runnin' ... all the way down to camp. We meet Willy and Dick at the gate, corral the bunch, and the problem is solved. Time for imposition of insult to injury. We catch them all, throw on pack saddles and load 'em up heavy ... four elk and two deer head out to the trailhead. Return trip, next day, with two hundred pounds of cubes, apiece, back to camp! Then plenty of unpaid overtime over the next week hauling the next group of hunters all over these mountains. Idle minds amid mountain hideouts become devil's workshops ... .

As for old Bone Rattlin' Pal, he got a double dose of horse cubes, a break from the meat run and turned out down by the creek. With his buddies, he could feast on lush grass and contemplate his eventual retirement.

A couple years later, it became evident that those long trail miles were taking a toll on those old-timers. So, I sold four, Pal among them, to a dude rancher who was trustworthy. What better means of hedging the odds for longevity than good feed, mountain splendor and a regimen of light workouts packing guests to favorite haunts?

Ten years hence, I was at the rancher's home place, helping him get caught up on the shoeing. First morning, he had 25 or 30 head tied up at the hitchrails, down below the cabins. Looking them over, there was familiarity. Seeing some of the prominent, old brands raised an eyebrow. Noted were several from local ranches. A few heads turned, and there was a loud snort. It was unexpected to come face to face with an old friend.

Another old friend from that same bunch was Tony, a thousand-pound gray, half Arab, half quarter horse. He stood about 15.2, but what he lacked in stature, got more than compensated for with heat and fire.

By the time I purchased the outfit, he was going on about

sixteen and had been all over that country, no doubt for the better part of a full decade. Most judges of horseflesh would likely claim that this one was over the hill, so to speak, as in beyond ten. Reality dictated otherwise with this character.

Wrangling off of him was an adventure every time you saddled up. We used to put him on picket, often within sight of the cook tent. When the wrangler or yours truly finished the 7:00 AM coffee and walked out of the dining tent, spurs aclangin', he'd immediately take notice and up would come his head from all that grass. He'd start in, dancing around on the end of that rope, literally fit for tying over what he knew was forthcoming. He'd start whinnying, snorting away until you got the lead untied and on the way to the hitchrail. Man, did he take a shinin' to those horse cubes.

I'd throw on the old bear trap, and when it came time for the bridle, he'd just reach over and clamp the bit. "No need for nonsense warming the damn thing up," he seemed to say ... "just wastes time!" So, we were off to the races. "Which way, today, Boss?" he'd ask. I'd give him one subtle bit of rein, and he was on point. We headed on downcountry to the lower meadows, where the outfit bunch often hung out that time in late season. Grasses there were well cured, maxed out in protein, and those nags weren't born yesterday. They'd get everything they could, that time of year.

We worked our way southwest, following horse tracks in the snow from the night before, when we turned out the rest of the dude string. We were trucking along at a slow trot, Tony sniffing the tracks and snorting, no doubt upon recognition of one or several of his buddies. After about two miles of this, we stopped, pausing to listen ... .

Tracks are fresher, now, and he's on point. Those radar ears are rotating, seeking any hint of metallic vibration. Time to roll one, the smoke playing circles in the steam of horse breath. It's colder this morning ... frostier than last night, and we hear the honkers, answered by a lone coyote catching mice along the creek. Must be about 10 degrees, as the hands start to protest in these worn-out leather gloves, and the ice along the creek cracks away.

We push on, the effort promoted by a slight touch of the spur: an elation, harmony with nature's remarkable work of acuteness. These four-legged angels can never cease to amaze. Twenty minutes later, we are amid fresher tracks, and his nose is into them, perusing for identity. Suddenly, we stop, the radars pointed forward. There are bells and horses ... seven head at the timbered edge of the far meadow.

We pick our way silently around them, gaining the extended timber and unmistakable scent. Time to disallow the reins, free all restraints and hang on, well mounted, for a hell-for-leather ride to perdition! Thanks, once again, to the real Boss for them bear traps!

By the early 1980's, and coming to the realization that those long trail miles to and from the camps were taking their toll on the horseflesh, I began making semiannual trips to Death Valley to pick up mules for the outfit. Having to double up on horses for the fall hunting was proving itself cost-ineffective, so the idea of an alternative in the form of hybrids began to hold merit. Mule teams and borax had gotten the attention of the entrepreneur. The notion was to prove itself viable over the next several decades, as the options afforded leaving nearly the entire strings of older dude horses in the camps, as opposed to repeatedly pounding them to mincemeat over the high passes. The mules, in spite of the long distances and hours, rarely lost more than about fifty pounds throughout the seasonal durations. The option ultimately proved itself so cost-effective that it warranted the consolidation of guides, clients and hunting horses in the mountains, overlapping the trips in proportion to trail time, with the same accommodated exclusively by the outfitter/packer and supply trains. Thus, traditional down time between trips was eliminated. The manifestation of four simultaneously operating hunts produced, remarkably, minimal daily pressures on the game populations, and so success ratios soared at top levels. Unprecedented statistics ensured protracted results in terms of repeat clients and references, both numbering well into the hundreds throughout a quarter-century of operation.

Knowledgeable guides, reliable dude horses and thirty-seven head of Mammoth mules had everything to do with terms of contribution to the merits. Those mules were a Godsend from heaven.

Now it is well known that there are quite a few more craftier hooligans among mules than among their counterpart equines. Those long-eared democrats assimilate a learning curve far more rapidly: in fact, like greased lightning, such that they earn their well-founded reputations. Rarely are they found to make the same error twice.

Perhaps it comes with entropy and the Second Law of Thermodynamics. Nature tends to seek paths of least resistance and gravitates to lower Eigenstates. The intelligence seems to originate from an innately endowed tendency to work towards making life easier. It is not unusual to drag a few colts up the trail, with light packs set to offer a getting-used-to process, and initially find them hammering a few trees enroute to wherever. But key is the fact that rarely will such persist and evolve into habit. Amid blowdowns, they rapidly pick up on careful foot placement, and the packer learns to look after them by counting individual feet amid critical spots, thus, accordingly, precision-adjusting rate of travel by the saddle horse. In aberrant sectors of especially gnarly blowdowns, on occasion, these characters will amuse by engaging in a finessed and artful jumping of the same, strategically timed in sync, such that the landing becomes coincident with the instant launch of a sequential counterpart. In long strings, this artfully finessed sequencing of coordinated virtuosity comports to collective genius which has never ceased to amaze. It becomes absolutely fascinating, engaging amid this training process and watching the wheels turn under those long ears! Poetry.

By the time of the '88 Yellowstone fires, those strings were well versed, and there was little they hadn't seen in all that country. One of the drainages we travelled enroute to the camps, offered a fairly long, narrow topography that had burned extensively, owing to the Mink Fire, from approximately the lower end to midpoint. Within a couple of years, the root networks of the scarecrow timbered remains were starting to give way, and enhanced by substantial winds, there were a lot of blowdowns. These were either already on the ground, or hangers in the making. Often, in strings of fourteen, maybe sixteen, head, those seasoned critters hammered the trails, day and night, to and from the camps. Recollection is virtually absent relative to more than a handful of incidents of having to stop, go back and retie setback, broken lines. Those critters proved themselves a formidably effective machine. Even unflappable.

On one occasion in early November, we were on the timbered portion of the old Pass Creek trail. Time was about 3:30, maybe 4:00 AM, and there were high winds, perhaps sixty to seventy mph.

The burned-out timber creaked and groaned eerily, amid the raging blasts, and periodically some of the stuff broke loose and came crashing down around us. Several hours of this, and all our nerves were shot to hell. Finally, down came a colossus with our name on it. Shattered timber crashed directly behind the lead, more between about #'s 6 and 7, plus some farther back. Everything came to a halt. And that's just where it stayed ... halted, as in stopped! I dropped the reins on Bandit, went back, anticipating a bloody mess, but all that was to be found amounted to a war zone of shards. Tall ears and benevolent eyes pointed in my direction. The sheath knife did its work, freeing them. Time to pull those demos out of the maze and get rolling again. In those days, demos of the two-legged variety were just learning how to complain, triangulate and play the victim. Not this four-legged cavalry. We rolled on through the wind tunnel from hell, pulling into camp about 9:00 AM without further incident.

Bandit and mules on the Pass Creek trail.

Long about the spring of 1983, a string of Mammoth mules came up for sale in the Death Valley region. It was time to crank up the old "struggle buggy" stock truck and git on down there, post haste, to have a look at them before some pot licker ran the table. Always good to get a few of the researchable preliminaries out of the way before the "official" inception of the game, so to speak. They turned out, it seemed, to constitute a high-class lot, bred via Mammoth jacks amid thoroughbred and quarter horse mares. Looking over about 70 head, it proved advantageous to bid on about 25 or so, subsequently load up 10, and drive on back to Wyoming. By choice, given the pertinent remoteness and terrain of the Thorofare Region, as well as the anticipated, relevant longevity issues, the opted-for candidates were mostly five- and six-year-olds.

Still, one can never be sure what he's got until the aforementioned get put to work. Packed and tied together for the first time, up the trail we went. The only seasoned critter in that particular string and on that day was the saddle horse, Rowdy. With mules, it turned out, he had neither rapport nor patience. At first those demos neither lined out nor paid the slightest attention to banging those packs against trees. They proceeded up that trail in a gaggle of major disorder, tangled leads and all. Needless to say, there were major train wrecks, ongoing, before, finally, all the chaos, and not the greenhorn cowboy, taught them to line out. The subject, by this time, was finally also starting to ascertain the merits of patience and quiet, and so the potential blue air and fumes thus remained, respectively, transparent and reticent. Better, of course, should those mountains harbor surreptitious listeners, eavesdropping out of "innocent" curiosity, to remain silent and be thought the fool, than to speak, thereby, removing all doubt; and know-it-all cowboys be damned.

Well, ok. Given a little time working among these characters, and, inevitably, some of their quirky traits start to surface. Take Red Cloud, for instance. He was 5 when hauled back from California. It became clear, early on, that he had some real issues. Generally deemed appropriate to worm these characters twice a year, and give them a 5-in-1 at least once over the same time frame, the regimen got followed meticulously by the organization ... however, not at all ritualistically, but, rather, tumultuously, by not just a few of the recipients. As for the aforementioned lop-eared democrat, early one morning at the base corrals, he left a clear impression that that wheels-turning brain box was not born yesterday.

Several of us were in the corral, making the rounds, generally catching the stock, injecting, paste-worming and turning the same back loose, all in practically one continuous motion. As we worked through the approximately 30 head, there were a few reluctant, who got snubbed to the center post and the issues forced, pretty much without inordinate difficulty. Mr. Cloud was, however, a different story.

As the three of us worked clockwise, imploding through the bunch toward the center, he maneuvered counterwise and peripherally, ears laid down and eyes askance, and as in surreptitiously, determined through sneaky and innocuous absence, to circumvent the process. Noting the aberrant pattern and concomitant devious glance, it became imperative to get this intractable character caught and tied. Cornering him, several of us got the culprit captured and in the process of snubbed up short, shot and wormer applied. However, those eyes went subsequently ballistic, and several rope burns on bewildered cowboys later, Mr. Cloud had, amid a broken halter and a jumped seven-foot corral, regained the stratosphere enroute to parts unknown. Incredulous, two of us saddled up and gave pursuit, following the tracks through adjacent BLM desert nearly to the next county. Days later we managed reinstatement, opting, in the future, for 'preemptive' chaw, assimilated with the feed, in lieu of the conventional worming chore, and a stouter chain halter as prerequisite for the '5-in-1' adventure.

He had other quirks, as well.

Once this born-yesterday cowboy got the bright idea to save time by making catching up the saddle horse among thirty, or so, head at the base corrals, an easier chore. Rowdy got turned loose, haltered, the lead detached and hanging off a handy post. Several of the mules offered a somewhat innocuous curiosity, waning in marginal attenuation, and in accord with the level of acceptance. Not Red Cloud. The intractable heathen wasn't about to let that one slide by. He took that whole issue as an affront and made a retaliatory game out of it. Latching onto the halter with clenched jaws and prominent incisors, he proceeded to drag Mr. Rowdy circuitously around and throughout the corral, much to the amusement of the entire clan and party. Before long, one recently and relatively ordered collection of demos had convened in emergency session and proceeded to instate societal disarrangement. Needless to say, this harebrained originator of animal farm had to quickly rethink the scatterbrained notion, contrived for enhancement, retrieve the halter and replace the same to its rightful location -- an empty nail back in the tack shed. So much for insurrection, popular vote and more than enough democracy for one day! At least this indulgence in the experimental failed to meet the criterion for irreversibility!

Well, in regard to Chief Red Cloud, the story had just begun.

Long about the spring of 1989, the organization succeeded in leasing a ranch near the trailhead on the South Fork. In short, this event proved itself a Godsend, for acquisition of the facility and location collectively resolved what had formerly constituted the necessity of running a fairly complex operation, literally, out of a snowdrift. In fact, locational convenience and enhancements to efficiency afforded the proprietor the chance to sleep, for once, thus inspiring the aspirant cowboy toward metamorphosing the option to lease into making an offer for purchase. Such wishful efforts proved themselves ill founded, however, and, as in fading with the sunset, so ultimately did the dream. Enough about wannabe renditions of cowboy vision.

Nevertheless, by 1989, the organization had acquired some 37 head of these red Mammoths, and amid this bunch of tall heathens and another string of 10, or so, saddle horses, Mr. Red Cloud proceeded to leave his mark.

Relative to chronology, he was pushing ten years, in the prime of life and springing those surprises on a daily basis. Clearly, the remainder of his colleagues were enjoying the process, especially when he figured out methods for unlatching gates, gaining privileged access to food-supply bunks, cube-storage racks and so on. It became almost impossible to leave the place unattended for even a few hours, for this aberrant stooge was virtually into anything mechanical, evidently simply for nothing other than the challenge, itself.

Well, one day I had to get to town to pick up critical last-minute supplies for a forthcoming trip. It was, by then, mid-July, and the pack trips were in full swing, with hired hands coming and going, guests arriving and the usual frenzy. The ranch, however, wound up temporarily vacant amid all the scrambling. Mr. Cloud was not about to let that one slide by, unmeddled.

The hands had just gotten the lawn next to the main house mowed, and it was a relief to see that chore out of the way, before I left for town. Charlie had retired the mower to the machine shed, closing the sliding door. A quick glance by the concerned to an adjacent pasture lent credence that all was well with 50, or so, head, and that all was ready for the forthcoming major trip ... .

Time to jump in the old truck, get to town and blitz the place for those supplies. The rig departs the ranch in a cloud of dust, and the pedal gets put to the metal all the way to town. In a frenzy of two hours, the shopping gets accomplished, and all is on the way back to home base.

Arrival proves itself disconcerting. Peaceful departure amid relative tranquility has undergone transformation to bedlam. Mr. Geronimo has managed to jump the perimeter fence, thus gaining entry to the residential sector. Of course, having patiently observed the grass-cutting episode, he's gone straight to the unlocked machine shed, succeeded in ingeniously retrosliding the door, thus gaining entry. Now he's dragged the mower out in front of residence and is proceeding vicariously with disassembly. Presently, he's got the engine cover off, and, with alacrity, three of the wheels discarded. The carburator is a twisted wreck, the distributor fragmented to atoms.

The concerned is livid with stress, so the old pickup now comes to life and gives him a few runs toward the jumped fence. Not the answer. Coming to a halt, it's time to inspect the damage and make assessment relative to salvage. That's dust in the wind, of course. In the meantime, Geronimo plays the stand off-and-observe game at thirty yards, the rotating ears and bright eyes lending a taunting aura to his otherwise self-assured nature. Amid the contemplation of subsequent actions, the ranch house phone rings; no doubt the guests calling to communicate their arrivals. I'm at the phone for several minutes' conversation. Upon return, the revelation is that Mr. G. has dragged the remains of the euthanized machine off into the South Fork, where to this day it remains under four feet of water. So much for trusting half-breed democrats ... .

Another, out of the same Death Valley string, that year, was

Houdini. Originally, the West Coast hands who worked on the ranch that sold him, called the character BJ, apparently after some disc jockey going back to the 1960's. "BJ the DJ,"* one might presume, had something to do with all that nonsense.

Anyway, it certainly took little time for BJ to wear out the original nomenclature and acquire a new one. That went for the welcome, as well. It began on approximately the third pack trip that summer. Slim, Kelsey and I were about to run 20 head into the South Camp in conjunction with a fishing-party family of four, coming for ten days.

Now those dual-purpose deals can be alright ... you git a jump on all those extra loads that have got to go to camp afore the time elk hunting season rolls around, the stock and hired help in shape and working well, plus extra cash from the proceeds of the pack trip. One thing for sure, though, is that the outfit better be well organized and have the majority of the kinks worked out, tall tales and cowboys be damned.

Some of the Death Valley bunch at the North Camp corral.

*By Stonewall Jackson, 1964.

Well, ok. It seemed, by this time that summer, we had things pretty well operating smoothly. It was the final week of July, the picket grass at our camps was still holding steady, and, thus far, the flies were not negatively affecting us. Actually, we were slightly ahead of schedule relative to the fall "pack ins." Consequently, with Dick looking after things in camp, and the remainder of us in town, the process called for Slim and Kelsey to git to the trailhead about daybreak, proceed with catching and saddling the stock, and for the boss to meet the clients for breakfast. It proved enhancing, a chance to appreciate the enthusiasm of this quality group, for an hour, prior to departing for the trailhead ... .

When all arrive, about 8:30, Slim and Kelsey have the whole outfit caught and most of them saddled. All the riding stock are ready, so we tie on slickers, give out sack lunches and fit stirrups to size. Following a brief safety demonstration, we begin packing the 20-mule train:

Well, once cowboys git to packing, seems like everything goes into overdrive. You can't be a cowboy packer without working like greased lightning and jerking hard those ropes and cinchas. Maybe it's because most cowboys won't tolerate too much scrutiny, likely owing to perusal at the careful level must produce flaws ... and as everyone knows, cowboys are perfect, or damn shore close to it! So, all of us went into frenzied packing mode, grabbing an "empty," tightening cinchas, tossing on the packs, pack cover and throwing some kind of hitch. I was trying to keep up with the rest of those hands, so wound up not paying any real attention to what else was going on, as in the situational-awareness department. That can prove to constitute bad business, at times.

Well, this time the culprit was BJ. He turned out to be one of the first packed, by yours truly, with white gas, if recollection is correct, and got led back to a corral post for retying. Packing up the remainder, we were joking around among ourselves and the guests, thus paying little attention to pertinent details. Long about twenty minutes later, amid leading a fourth critter back to the corrals for retying, it became noticeable an attenuation in the number that were tied. A modicum of perusal produced the realization that the number was none! The SOB's were all over the place, without halters, or without leads, or dragging leads and no breakaway ties. In fact, former breakaway ties were dunce-metamorphosed into breakaways, themselves, the ties be damned ... .

A few "What the hells?" later, and it becomes clear that Mr. Sneaky Politician, BJ, is the scandalous culprit, this go-around. Slim, now in the process of re-sizing the slid halter as in leather punching a few more slots, claims he'll show that no-good lop ear a thing or two. Kelsey recalls that at least once, the same goofball, a few weeks earlier, "inadvertently" flipped one of the gate latches at the ranch, letting some thirty head into the wrong pasture.

So, we catch up all the loose stock, much to the amusement of our guests. "Must be lending credence and enhancing confidence among a new group of clients, this losing half the transport before the commencement of a trip into grizzly country," is the latest in profound contemplation.

The family's ten-year-old shouts, "Why don't you call him Hoodiny? Don't you think, Boss?"

"Yeah, good thinkin' kid! ... call for the vote!"

Amid lots of horselaughter, everyone raises a hand.

"Any dissention? ..."

"The I's have it, then ... done deal!"

"Kelsey, bring Hoodiny over ... . One of us is going to lead this character. There won't be any further escapes on this trail, at least not today!"

A safety briefing, and we're ready to go up the trail.

Snowflake was a lease horse who came to the outfit back in about the 1983-84 era. He was an Appaloosa, white in background color, with lots of gray splotches. That marvel was an absolute prince of a saddle horse, standing about 15.3 and weighing nearly 1200 lbs. He was also hell on wheels to shoe.

Amazing how a totally dog-gentle equine, more than ready to let just about anyone brush, saddle up, bridle and ride anywhere, day or night, can metamorphose into an unholy terror when it comes to foot handling. In fact, foot approaching, in any conventional manner anticipated, proved itself 'endemische verboten!' Well, upon making the lease deal for additions to the dude string, late that summer, the old piker who owned them cut a pretty good deal. We stipulated that I would have to shoe the bunch. Yep, that vaquero wasn't born yesterday. Clearly, one of the predominant reasons was Snowflake, for the others turned out to be not so bad in the nailing-on-iron department.

So, ok. We had eight head in the round corral, with seven of them all done. Slim had had a little trouble initially with him, so we put the reticent on hold, rather than get the whole bunch stirred up over nonsense. Finishing the remainder, we decided to gang up on the recalcitrant. Tied off to one side, and as we approached with the tools, he was giving the eye. That glare was none too friendly:

We scotch him up and proceed to rasp, shape the hinds and get them nailed on. With some chaotic jumping around, we manage with a pair, marginally fitted. Now for the fronts. Of course, everyone knows you can't get the fronts shod, with a scotched-up hind, at least on the same horse, standing. Benevolent logic might suggest that dropping the hinds would appeal to the horse's better side and produce concurrent acceptance relative to the fronts. Not with this cayuse. Attempts at raising a front, either side, produce immediate retaliation, accomplished via a balance on two offside limbs, concomitant with a synchronized blindside lateral delivery via an onside hind. Not a good practice for even the most hard-headed of old-timer cowboys ... .

Well, dammit, the ground is concrete hard and full of snarly, sharp rocks, so we're not going to be able to throw the goofball. Time for the twitch. Long story short, that works for a while, but over the full term, you got to apply the same with finesse. Too much torque, the lip goes numb, then distraction diversion goes abruptly

south, and he's out for blood, again. Too little in the twist department, and the effects are minimal, with much the same in retribution.
Kelsey appears not to have gotten the finer points of the message,
so we graduate to the war bridle. Suppose it's time yours truly actually does something like handle that chore, while Slim goes to fitting, nailing, and Kelsey to shaping. By the end of all this,
Snowflake wants less of the war bridle and more of the shoes. Now
we're all thinking, dammit, why the heck don't they invent a few of
these appys with darker feet!

Well, ok, that chore done, we're friends once again ... .

Somehow, wrangler Willy missed out on most of these shoeing adventures, at least for a while, that year. Anyways, that saga
continued a bit longer, and into the fall, to be more precise. Seems
as though some of the Snowflake episodes got discussed at length
up in camp, and a few of the stories passed down over the years.
Finally, late one fall season, a few years down the pike, Willy got
fed up with listening to all the rest of us and decided to produce one
that might top all the former ones.

He'd made friends with one of our hunter clients who used
to work for the railroad in one of the East Coast states. Apparently,
they had used some sort of chemical flares for night-work signaling
back there ... and just by coincidence, this jokester had brought several with him in his duffel for the trip. Just in time for Halloween
episodes, Thorofare camp, circa 1985.

Late fall at the South Camp, prior to the 1988 Yellowstone fires.

Halloween was, of course, traditionally our last evening of hunting, given the duration of elk season and inclement weather, so the next morning we would commence with pulling out the camps and calling it a year.

Consequently, that night, we had virtually all the stock, or about forty head, tied up to every hitchrail, corral post and anything else horizontally solid or vertically anchored, in circumference of proximity to camp ... .

Given the final night of a successful season, most of us are indulging in a few festive spirits with longtime clients of several years, when vociferous laughter emanates from the corrals. In fact, clamorous bedlam seems to be undergoing transformation into horselaughter, metamorphosing into the frenzied variety, as of the engine-run-too-hard variety. Horrified and packing iron, I'm met at the entry to the dining tent by Willy, returning breathlessly from the corrals, briefly unable to contain himself, let alone speak intelligibly.

"Boss, you aren't going to believe this. It's Snowflake ... he's done it again! You've got to come and see this!"

By now, the hunters are curious, so setting aside all indulgences, we head out to the hitchrails. In the pitch black, forty pairs of eyes reflect the bonfire, sparks rising into the void above, lending a wolflike paleolithic aura amid tall timber. But from the center, and shining as in beacons among ambient radiance, the brighter spots, long mane and swishing tail, the only horse in our care, ever, to glow in the dark.

"Happy Halloween, my friends!"

# Chapter 11, "Nomo Me Impune Lacesset"

A summer or two after lending Joe a hand on those summer pack trips in the Yellowjackets, the next step in the progression was to hire on with Jake and Joe for the fall season. Tom was taking only a few elk hunters that year and doing most of the guiding himself. Consequently, he lent out his mostly borrowed string of stooge mules, and in whatever the deal was he and Joe worked out, the concerned got somehow included.

By this time the stooge string had come a long way in terms of trail miles, bear and hornet episodes, elk-packing disasters and alarms going off in the dark amid dude-packed, duffel-by-installment events. They really had become a seasoned string, and having had some to do with the assimilation process, there was justifiable pride in them. They had pretty much seen it all by that time, or at least so everyone thought.

Well, we started early that year, in terms of preparation for the fall season. Joe and Jake had managed to book some 50-plus elk hunters for the Middle Fork camps, and that meant that we had to take in some 120 loads of staples, horse cubes, propane, white gas, camp accessories, tents, cots and all the stuff necessary for pertinent operations, prior to the inception. So, in late June we shod the 12 head of demos all the way around, and right after the Fourth of July, the mission for the concerned became, "Git up that trail and head fer the Kitchen Creek Camp."

It's a fair piece back into that country, certainly in excess of 30 miles up that old Middle Fork trail. This turned out to be one of those drier years, as well, 'long about the mid '70's, and perhaps a decade or so precursor to those big Yellowstone fires. Anyways, sometimes along with dryness can come a bad year for snakes, as in rattlers. This particular year proved itself the worst I can remember ... .

Ok, so it's 5 July, and we're on those switchbacks, climbing high above the North Fork. 10:00 AM, and it's pushing 85 F. Nevertheless, after the long, do-nothing winter, it was much better to be horseback and hearing those rock-clacking-away mules pulling up the trail. Wearing diamonds, the raw-boned, old string looked pretty good. We took a few breathers before pulling over the top and into the Middle Fork canyon.

Now back to the snake department. As most certainly much of the readership must be well aware, these Rocky Mountain variants of diamond-backs and prairie critters are known as timber rattlers. They feed on squirrels, small rabbits and mice, laying cunning ambushes amid fallen logs and rotted stumps, purposely occupied adjacent the habitual thoroughfares of their prey. They are masters of the lay-in-wait strategy. Contrary to ignorant opinion, these marvels bear their young, thus nesting in proximity to water, as well as a viper's crawl away from drier areas incorporating larger flat rocks for sunning.

This critter is known also as Crotalus horridus Linnaeus, and is truly a viper in every sense. The triangular head is of perfect design for hunting and laying ambushes. Actually, the vertical pupils offer peripheral coverage to an extent of 200 degrees, and so amid the semi-arid desert, a decided advantage over perhaps 60-degree bilateral tunnels of its prey become readily apparent. This one is quite dangerous, owing to a particularly potent venom of high yield, and unusually long fangs for injection. When disturbed or threatened, he'll raise the tail and generally rattle away. The venom accomplishes its work owing to hemotoxic, cytotoxic and neurotoxic attributes of the endemic protein chemical structures. Relative to humans, however, he seems to prefer long-term rattling to combat, thus apparently showing predisposition for conservation of venom, thereby enhancing availability for food acquisition, and this constitutes, in the general sense, a saving grace.

Now, clearly, these characters seem to prefer slopes with southern exposure, and in order to accomplish the logistical balancing act concerning acquisition of water, foodstuffs and bearing their young, they'll migrate. There appear to exist two tiers supporting this phenomenon.

The first occurs over a 24-hour basis, as in a daily routine of all-night and early-morning nesting, in relative proximity to water. This is followed by subsequent movement to higher elevation and warmer flat rocks for sunning, revitalization in preparation for a third phase of hunting. Most often ambushes are laid at elevations diminutive to the latter, but at a higher level than the nests.

The second tier constitutes a more seasonal migration, as in a general population-wide movement to diminutive-locale hibernation dens.

It will be the former transition that will drive the equation relating to pertinent details forthcoming:

Well, ok. Going up that trail proved itself not without a few trepidations and woeful apprehensions, temporary in nature, however. Jake had offered well-intended precautionary warning concerning the extent of potential for rattlers. "Watch yer topknot in that damn Stoddard Creek," he had stated. "They kin be thick as fleas in there, some years, Pard."

So, it was time to be on the lookout.

"Watch yer topknot in snake country."

Now, that's not going to be exactly like you might be lookin' fer, as in an old grey diamondback. Rather, these timber variants tend to present more of a yellow or tan brown, possessing chevron-like cross bands instead of the diamonds. Because the shades blend well with the surroundings, prudence dictates the utility of keying on the geometric irregularities of the chevrons, to optimize detection. With that cognition in place, it became straightforward, with some practice, to locate the aforementioned, and they began, with some regularity, showing up amid hideouts off the trail, at the crossings, and even in trees among the branches. Remarkably, it soon became evident that these critters were proving themselves fully capable of climbing the trunks for laying ambush, obviously to squirrels. Reflecting on the peripheral dilemma, the Stoddard Creek population would soon be demanding full and foreboding, multidimensional concentration.

Well, by noon she was really heating up on that mountainside, the pack train sweating over the taxations of a first trip. A couple of times, high above the Middle Fork, it proved time for a temporary breather, to facilitate the flowing sweat to subside and physiology to diminish. Good we weren't loaded all that profusely, given lower-elevation latent attenuations of fitness among winter pastures. There is also a tendency for inattentively and improperly balanced packs to roll on soft mutton-withered stock which might possess a few extras in the weight department. So, during halts it merits the packer to pay close attention to details of stability, especially on those early trips. Clearly, the situation remedies as the season progresses, concomitant with loss of weight and generally improving issues of progressive fitness.

Alright, we're trundling along rather well this early afternoon, cutting a few switchbacks, and, in spite of the laboring efforts of the string, all are accommodating a pretty decent sense of efficiency in motion, as in rhythm, syncopation and long, swinging ears. That comports to a sense of mellow relaxation on the part of the demos, and every cowboy packer worth his salt looks for this signatory demeanor, relative to assessment concerning a collective impression of well-being. All is precisely what one charged with ultimate responsibility hopes for, as in balance, poise and equanimity. The confirmation advances the notion of a greater sense of relief that a collective psyche of the population gravitates in a direction conducive to harmony. Quite unlike whims of experimental chaos offered by not-so-enlightened, scandalous, out-of-touch, modern-day politicians. Bilegged self-serving fools jump where four-legged veterans are reticent to tread. The consequences of mindless manipulation, fueled by incessant reinventions of illusion. Mein Gott!

Remarkably, one learns to perceive, transmit and otherwise communicate the sense of relative compatibility, or, for that matter, a lack of the same, through the lead rope, itself. Thus, a well-developed sense of telepathy preempts an absolute necessity for ongoing daylight visual scrutiny, and most importantly, to an extent, replaces the same during the hours of travel throughout darkness. Well developed, this presence facilitates safe and viable operations over extended periods and great distances ... .

Travel is perpetual, day or night. Telepathy is key.

Well, ok, 'long about early afternoon we drop down off a few switchbacks, heading for the West Fork of Stoddard. Midway, it is time to tighten a few britchens, raise the downhill side pack on Larry and retighten two cinchas. Precautionary notions relative to what's coming ... steeper downhill and more switchbacks. Finally, amid profuse dust and unsettled locusts, we hit the bottom, cross the Main Fork of Stoddard and gain the North Fork ... .

Back in the 1930's the economy in these parts wound up depressed owing to the 1929 cratering of the stock market. FDR offered remedy by proceeding with the New Deal. The intention was to counter the negative condition by putting our citizens to work, so to speak. So, numerous projects got proposed, and various facilitating agencies came into existence. Among them was the Civilian Conservation Corps, or CCC, which received the mandate to build a system of trails throughout the Rockies and various mountain ranges, thus to provide administrative access, as well as recreational diversion for the public. Well, old Franklin D. was pretty savvy, as this effort, among many, served to achieve acceptable levels of employment and get the Nation producing again. All enhanced the successful effort in bringing the Country out of the Great Depression. That's how many of the present-day trails in these here mountains initially got built.

However, most of the same originally were game trails, used by deer, elk and bighorns, indigenous to the various regions, for travel between feeding areas, water sources and, in some instances, between summer and winter ranges. Often times, these amounted to a series of sparse game trails separated by relatively difficult, or easy, terrain where travelling animals tended to disperse. So when the CCC came along, they went to work connecting the same and augmenting a more permanent-like structure, which much improved the terms of continuity.

Most of the endemic routes were originally disjointed game trails.

No one can, with any credibility, contest the efficacy of work done by these men in relation to the trails, themselves, for most of them, well weathered, endure to this day. Yet, at times, it seems as though there are grounds for questioning the wisdom of the placement.

Take this Stoddard Creek trail, for instance. Back in the 70's, it was a good route, most certainly offering safe travel at about 3 miles per hour for any reasonably fit pack train. A few blowdowns over the winter got sawed out in the early summer, and, barring unusually adverse early-fall weather, she was ok through November.

This author never met any of the men who built the entity 40 years prior, but one issue is for certain. While they built an excellent trail, it was not well oriented. Damned if it didn't get set right smack orthogonal to the daily short-term timber rattler spring, summer, fall migration routes among sunning, nesting and ambushing sectors. Anything or body travelling this route, day or night, would, by design, encounter predictably statistically viable densities of rattlers on an ongoing basis. There could be no avoidance of such negative probability, given the configurations of the trail, and the placements relative to the interfacing drainages.

So, the author is, to this day, eager to meet a few of these folks who put this marvel in place. Perhaps they indulged in a little of the old sauce, from time to time, and thus preferred to keep their talents of ingenuity bottled up, so to speak. Maybe, there were few or no timber rattlers back up the Middle Fork in those days, although that seems doubtful. The locals used to claim they were always prevalent along the Salmon. It might even be that the founding father socialist democrats of old contrived this experiment for the hell of it, waiting, thus, to derive any insightful results. Sounds quite like their present-day descendants.

Well, ok, so we are heading up the West Fork of Stoddard, clickety-clack. The stooges, having gotten tanked up on water at the North Fork crossing, are travelling well, but seem apprehensive. This ain't their first rodeo, and when these characters have been through a few, the tendency leans toward the development of a sixth sense. The cowboy packer can be well advised to take heed of such radar premonition signs, and lend all credence to what might be coming. At times the signs can be subtle. The forthcoming, relative to the imminent, would be anything but:

The place turned out to be in the shadows, much of the day just out of reach of the sun's rays, which now, by late afternoon, were cut off by the divide into Color Creek. The locale, in spite of the warmth and dryness of an otherwise pervasive desert-like parchness, had by now taken on a sultriness, which had made belabored even normal efforts at respiration. One could see it in the stock, heaving away up the trail, trying to sustain the pace, so time to slow by a third for compensation. Even Nitro, the ultimate in fitness, seemed to show gratitude for the gesture. And so, the rhythms of the string drew their melodics from more basal tones, as the originators pounded the rocky course.

With the reduced pace, the mind began its insidious course of acceleration, as in the devil's workplace. Recalling Jake's warning, the imagination played havoc with hanging moss, moving shadows among serrated jackpine stumps and stirrings in the tree bark. The visions proceeded involuntarily with laser focus upon every detail along that perfidiously invasive route. Even the rocks grew eyes, the pine needles, fangs, those sabres lashing out amid the dark forested irregularities. The space assumed a pungent odor of darkness and the macabre, the timbered starkness emanating the effects of ghastly, raw-boned scarecrows, contemplating ambush. We pounded up the long, dark tunnel to perdition.

Viciously, I forehanded the face, thus shocking the wanderings of discipline out of mind's consciousness. Then, abruptly, Nitro jolted to a halt, snorting loudly, the ears rivetted forward, lasered to the slithering four-footer ... .

He was mean and lean, mottled, and wearing the dark chevrons. I'm off of Nitro, eyeing the three-inch, four-foot club limb at forehead level for assassination. One snap off that jackpine, and it would perform execution with desired effect.

The landing is on coiled madness, the target's acquisition partner in co-conspired ambush. The rattling goes from quiet to raucous extreme in a second's fraction, and, unsheathed, show vicious sabres, drawn savagely, now fiendishly slicing the thankfully tall rawhide boots. Nitro is through the roof, as is this undisciplined, poor excuse of a cowboy, and when both alight, the former is hammering away with two hinds in retrograde. Now Mr. Horridus is hung up around the left boot spur, so down comes the right, which pins the front section at about the third chevron, to the rocky trail. Time to pull the sheath knife from the scabbard, years prior inadvertently rivetted to the lateral side of the boot, itself. Remarkable to have possessed such foresight.

Amazingly, born-yesterday cowboy has remembered to sharpen the weapon, days prior, so in short order, Mr. Viper is in sections, writhing away, but with sabres now lacking structure for leverage. To this day, there is indelibly printed upon the slate of consciousness, the image of exacting vengeance in that fiendish, hellish stare, rivetted, chilling and haunting, which he presented as I walked away.

"Nomo me impune lacesset!" One could not help but assimilate the vibes.

Now for his partner in conspiracy. With difficulty, the limb snaps off, but adrenalin prevails. Number two is up the trail, Nitro off a few yards, snorting barbarously. The viper crawls, then stops, coils, rattling profusely, as Nitro paws the ground. The knife is resheathed, so out comes the six. Reluctance to use it, however, on account of the stock, which, thus far, is holding intact. The limb can accomplish its deadly work without inviting the chaos of a train wreck.

So, time to go to calculated smashing, and the limb is effective. Mr. Horridus II proceeds with driving those sabres, but gets hammered, as well. Finally, he's off and running, down the hillside and headed for the creek. Critical to follow, yet prudently and not too closely, for he may have a gang of mafiosi company, as in Yep! Now, amid profuse brush, rotted-out downfall and more sliderock along the creek, there's an entire nest. Must be ten or twelve, and as Mr. Horridus gains entry, they all go into frenzied concert. The buzzing goes on the increase, harmonic vibrations rising to crescendo, and to a point of the monstrous and the satanic. The shadows, themselves, now become pervasively vindictive ... venomous. Not the time for playing hero. Shattered, it's time to exit this incestuous fire pit, regain the trail, and walk back to Nitro. Number one has finally expired fully, but that heinous, sabres-locked, glare endures.

To this day, I watch the backtrack, regardless of venue or nature of context.

Back in the early eighties, I got to making a lot of night runs into the Thorofare camps. The reasons were varied, but most prominent among them came down to an ongoing infusion of good horses into the riding string. Several possessed the attributes of superior night vision, steady nature, stamina and aptitude for the long haul. I wanted to take advantage of the state of the art, you might say, so generally after packing up about sundown, up the trail we went.

There were other advantages, as well. Among them was the improbability, amid difficult terrain, switchbacks, catwalks, creek crossings and the like, of running into an oppositely travelling pack train. For whatever the reasons, almost no one purposely rode the trails in the dark, and so the option provided an advantage of ex-clusivity rarely encountered throughout daylight hours.

Furthermore, it seemed as though the mule trains travelled more efficiently after dark. Temperatures were generally milder, at least throughout the summer months, and rodent-like wildlife seemed less active, thus facilitating a less-intruded mental process-ing by the livestock. It seemed as though, 'long around two hours, or so, into the march, most of them put the ritual on automatic pilot, and simply mellowed out all the way to camp. And so, quite often, arrival could be predicted within a few minutes of 5:00 AM ... North camp, South camp ... it didn't seem to matter.

It was, however, necessary to go well prepared up that long, lonesome ... as in Hank Williams' "Lost Highway."* Best to have those packs well balanced, perhaps to within a half-pound differen-tial, or even closer, my friend. Pads had better be applied in dou-bles, and set just right, three inches forward of the bars. Cinchas have got to be tight, but not too much so, with latigos put up and not swinging about. Breast collars and britchens require near-per-fect adjustment, or you'll be sorry to see a few sores, next AM. Best to pad them with fleece, in the form of extra insurance. Further, you'll want to have them halter buckles in the right notch if you want the convention intact for the coming hour.

If you take the job seriously, pardner, you'll learn quickly how to judge the level of contentment by ascertaining the collective dis-

*By Leon Payne, 1948.

position through the lead rope. The innovations of communication supplant the visual, amid the blues on dark-moon nights amongst the hoot owls.

Well, ok. This chapter is supposed to be more about horses and mules, so guess it's time to git along toward the punch line. Long about the late summer of 1983, I got into one helluva horse wreck. Some renegade heathen I was trying to ride blew up in the slide rock and put the aforementioned in the turf, as in underneath the horse. None too bright on the part of the rider, yet, in short, that turned out to be a blessing ... .

Following a two-day convalescence, I encountered a good friend: that is, a real one with the best of intentions, who wound up lending his pride and joy for the rest of the season. This one turned out to have all that his predecessor had lacked ... above all, the best of night vision, steadiness and plenty of bottom. He showed good savvy working around the mules, which took a shining to him almost immediately. By the end of the season, such was the level of attachment to "Old Smoke," that I made a substantial offer to his owner relative to purchase.

"Nothing doing!"

But Charlie was a true friend. Smoke had a twin brother, eight years old, and Charlie made proper introductions to the neighboring rancher. Long story short, I topped out Dusty, rode him for an hour, and made the same offer. "Deal."

Going up that long, lonesome trail.
10,500' Deer Creek Pass.

128

So, in going up that old trail, back then, often Dusty was the saddle horse, and he most certainly proved to be among the best. At sixteen hands and nearly 1200 pounds, he was stout enough to hold those setbacks on their haunches. In a jam, he was as steady as concrete, showed no fear of bears, or much else, for that matter, and his night vision proved to be at least as good as Smoke's. Seemed like he got a kick, pun intended, out of those prankster mules, Red Cloud, Hoodiny, and some of the stooges, when the packs were off. When there was time, it was gratifying watching them goofball around in the corral.

Well, the traditions of old cowboys die hard, if ever at all. Much worse and less likely for wannabe cowboy packers. The old-timers never admitted to carrying flashlights relative to night work, but in the early years, and in company of a few of those ornery characters back in the 60's, an occasional one of those gadgets did come out under certain conditions. Paramount among them was secrecy.

"Shhh - Keep this one under your hat, pard, lest yours truly be shot at sunrise over the sacrilege."

Well, the same might, with reservations, be said in reference to old-timer packers; but no such piker would ever admit to, much less be seen, making even brief use of such technology, nevertheless, jammed among a few diminutive, worn-out molars, thus freeing up the hands to jerk those cinchas.

Ach, Mein Gott! Impossible to imagine what fate likely would befall the poor gent who might be caught, at some point of weakness, making use of such higher-grade technology as a miner's headlamp ... for trail work, and with packstrings?! That kind of device was originally intended for use with those new-fangled brain buckets the technocrats have recently been jawing about ... and plastic ones at that!

Well, much to antiquated consternation as well as disavowal, yours truly received one of those contraptions as a gift from well-meaning family members. There was no clue as to what to do with the damn thing. Certainly it would never pass muster to be caught, red-handed, with the foul object. Without fail, from camp or the trail, perverted and contrived stories about it and its newly acquired operator would travel like greased lightning to every bar, lounge and cowboy hangout from Cheyenne to Jackson Hole. Then there'd be

Burnin' daylight off the Wedge.

hell to pay for the next thirty years. No living that one down. Qwatsch!

Now I was in a real jam. Had to show appreciation, somehow, to family, but couldn't put on any public displays amid the traditional culture. So, I crammed the damn thing clear down in the bottom of a saddlebag, batteries and all, and forgot about it, with the intent of proceeding with resurrection, should any family show up, unannounced, at the trailhead ... .

October proves itself a revelation. It's gotten colder, with Thorofare midnight temperatures dropping into the mid-teens. I'm riding Dusty, and we're pulling a string of ten or twelve down through a snarly deadfall portion of trail about fifteen miles out from south camp. It's been spitting snow most of the night, not really cutting loose, but threatening to. Wind's been building, as well, and ominous creaking of burned-out lodgepoles lends credence that a few more weeks of this, and it'll be time overdue to vacate the arctic icebox. Father Time talking, I guess.

There's just a sliver of moon showing from time to time amid those intermittent clouds there in the fast lane. She's dark as the inside of an Angus bull, out there. Time to go back, again, and check all them packs and cinchas, just to make sure that all is well before the final run into camp. Another five to six hours, and if the luck holds, one can sleep with the fishes.

Well, ok. As in ground tie, I drop the reins on Dusty, who snorts, and goes to chawing some old dead grass just off the trail. Out comes the jag light, turned on and jammed between a few teeth. First few packs look good, but the cinch on number four is slack. I'm reefing on it when out goes the light.

"Hm, bulb must have gone under."

Time to sit down and fit in the spare. In a few minutes the object's replaced, but with a bright flash, it flares out.

"Shorting out, somehow, I guess."

"Another day ( or night! ) in paradise. Now what?"

I'm cussing technology, in general, and specifically the maker of this piece-of-junk jag light, when, pun intended, the bulb, as in thinking box of yours truly, goes on. In short order, I'm thanking all the invisible, covered up, as in cloudy, stars above the entire Thorofare Country, for that brain-bucket piece of technology in the saddlebag. This time, and quite carefully, the apparatus is exhumed from the state of dormancy, and attached to my jumped-on old hat.

Damned if she doesn't fit!

Now let's see about this here lithium battery, which seems to go rather nicely right into a left coat pocket, and the switch ... . Holy cats and hell's bells!

The whole country lights up! Now the mules are all snorting, braying and carrying on. Their glowing eyes are all staring as though the entire democratic convention is in session ... or is it impeachment proceedings? Time to switch off the lithium and call things to order! What can one say when speechless ... ?

Well, the stock took a little time getting used to all that glare, but seemed grateful for its sparing use by the perpetrator. The remaining hours enroute to camp passed easily and without incident. Needless to say, a mile short of camp, that dark night, I, most grateful, meticulously stowed the life-saving object back to the bottom of a fastidiously rearranged saddlebag.

Now much the wiser, yet still reluctantly recalcitrant, we shall proceed:

Kelsey was an interesting sort of bird. He worked many years for the outfit, for nearly all of its twenty-five-year duration. He was a horseman, par excellence, only superseded in terms of accomplishment, by his talents at spinning yarns and spreading rumors. He was well connected, all the way south to as far as Cheyenne, and west to Jackson Hole and Afton. He had family all over the state, and in parts of Idaho, as well.

He and Slim, both, were well bound by cowboy traditions.

Ya took yer hat off in front of women, unless out of doors, and did the same upon entering the cook or dining tent, as in social graces.

The tack tent was a different story. God help the wet-behind-the-ears horse wrangler who left the handle of the coffee pot too close to the radiating stove pipe in the dining tent. That poor son-of-a-gun got dragged off to the tack tent, or worse, the lodgepoles, for a good heart-to-heart lecture. If the transgression persisted, and I never heard rumors relating to a subsequent installment, retaliation, promised, would be imminent and abrupt. Clearly, no cowboy wrangler I ever knew allowed curiosity to get the better, thus to test

October at the South Camp.
Texas Panhandle, upper right.

132

the waters of perdition.

One substantive difference of note existed between the two, Kelsey and Slim, relative to societal issues, however. Slim had little family, and only a handful of friends. Like Kelsey, he was an excellent horseman. Further, he kept camp business under his hat. Even when hitting town and tying one on, he could be depended upon to keep quiet when folks asked "innocent" questions pertinent to the outfit. Oh, he'd carry on about the Thorofare, alright, but when it came down to "nuts and bolts," he was totally reliable. Slim rode for the brand. Kelsey liked to spin a yarn or two about life up there, and he was known for the incredible speed at which his yarns, true or false, reached every podunk cowboy hovel, far and wide. Family ties, I guess.

One of the issues was, however, that stories contrived, or related, innocently enough, wound up decreasingly recognizable in proportion to distance from the storyteller. Like the time in the mid-80's, for example, when a couple of us flare-gunned some unsuspecting pest grizzly which kept, on a nightly basis, coming into camp and interrupting beauty sleep. Reality was that the bear got pretty well singed, ran off and left us alone for the remainder of hunting season. That was pretty much how I heard Kelsey tell the story, embellished a little, perhaps, most of the time in the local establishments.

However, what subsequently came out, after those effects made the rounds to Jackson, Cheyenne, etc., was that we'd caught the bear on fire, and that, turning tail, he'd run up the ridge and flamed the entire Thorofare Country. Years later, the story continued to reap its remarkable harvest. By the early 90's, the Yellowstone fires had gotten retroapplied, with rumors, among the local establishments, giving us the dubious honor of having started the ecological disaster. To this day, some of us still walk on egg shells, thinking that, in time, some concerned jackass might proceed to take the whole deal seriously, and seek restitution on behalf of Friends of the Tree Bark. I guess you can't fix stupid, but thanks to the Boss that statutes of limitations eventually do run out, as in thirty-plus years.

Well, yours truly was in one heckuva dilemma. At the near end of the trail, depending upon who showed up, I was applauding the merits of lithium lamps and batteries. At the camp end, the occasion was to deny, or at least obfuscate, the same, all for the merits of cowboy tradition. For quite some time, there was quandary pertinent to resolution of this Saturday night two-step. The relevant question came down to how does cowboy Pete sustain tradition, and simultaneously take advantage of legitimate technological advances. The old-timers said, "Ya can't have it both ways, Pard."

Well, perhaps there is a way. You might have to compromise the judgment system, itself. One way of doing so can begin with giving some of the more afflicted adherents enough rope. This can be accomplished figuratively, or as in the real Mc Coy ... all the same. Ultimately, the sanctimonious are prone to hanging themselves ... .

I recently heard rumors flying around, as in Kelsey ( or was it Willy? ) that some damn piker cowboy had won a prominent case in the courts over similar issues. The guy was some sort of business owner, who got too big for the britchen, so to speak, and began cutting "too hefty" a slice out of the pie. A little success can be a dangerous thing, and jealousy can get to the wrong heads.

Well, long story short, the cowboy's opposition pulled in quite an assortment of sabotaging agents, witnesses and the like, and as in "Hurricane," proceeded to incorporate criminal indictments, conspiratorial efforts and the like, to achieve disbarment. But with all that contrived stuff, the separately mandated endemic legal processes achieved categorically conflicting orthogonal results, pertinent to, in essence, the same charges. Thus, all that latitude in approach, compromised the legal system, itself. Too much of that old rope, it would seem.

Ok. I felt sorry for that poor piker cowboy, for then with the technological issue looming large between camps and the trailheads, and the predicaments clearly analogous, something had to be done. So, looking for a bit of mischief, I thought about giving Mr. Kelsey, the self-appointed judge, jury, investigator and press, in most matters, all the line he wanted, and then some.

Ok, half a mile short of camp, one dark-moon October night, that fall, out from the saddlebag came that technological marvel. I was riding Dusty, and by that late in the season, he had lost a little weight, the miles were wearing a bit thin and he had become quite mellow, especially thirty-plus miles into the long trail. He was a relatively trusting character, used to this rider ... and, so, it was possible to get away with pretty much anything around him ... as in I once shod him, all fours around, completely in the dark ... mess with his ears, give him the worming stuff, the five-in-one shot and most everything else.

So, it was a fairly easy job, fitting the lithium technology, adjusting the straps, and getting the semblance of illumination mechanism squarely mounted on top of his brain box. Now granted, he objected some, at first, but a little talking and conning by means of a handful of molasses cubes, and he came around rather well.

Well, I'm sure the reader has, by now, caught on as to what's coming, but I'll relate the remainder of this tall one, anyways ... .

Long about 4:30 AM, we were a bit early arriving in camp. The hands and cook were up, anticipating the pack train arrival, and most of them saw us pull in. They all joined at the corrals, thus helping to get the stock tied to hitchrails, trees and whatever else was handy. Dick had coffee ready, and it seemed as though everyone offered a good word ... .

Ok, so it wasn't long before I could see Slim, lending an eye to that cayuse of mine. He rolls a smoke, sets that lantern jaw, and now his eyes are in this direction. ( "What the hell, Boss?" )

I return the glance, putting up a single finger, a grinful smirk signaling the intent. Slim returns the gesture, and we go to unpacking.

With a couple of lights hung, I stare over the withers of the mule just unpacked, watching Kelsey working over in the direction toward Dusty. Now he's onto discovery. Slim is vibrating, trying to stifle the coming horselaughter, covering all with efforts on behalf of the work ethic. So, we managed to get through all of it without letting the cat out of the bag, Willy and Dick following suit, sort of just going along for the ride, shall we say.

A night or two later, we packed up the meat train with six bull elk and a couple of mule deer, and I left for the trailhead with fourteen head. This time, and quite visibly, Slim gave me a hand, fitting the technology to Dusty, and I pretended to be quite fastidious about making sure that all of it was fully engaged, upon departure.

Next day, shortly after the stock was unpacked, unsaddled, watered, fed and kicking back at the base corral, and the game quarters dropped off at the local processor, the home phone rings in Cody. It's one of my outfitter friends, calling clear the hell from

Jackson.

"What the hell, pard? Cowboys don't use a flashlight in the mountains! You don't use a light with a horse! What kind of worthless excuse of a hand are you becoming, anyways?"

"No, Bob, yer not getting it. I don't use a flashlight ... and never have. It's the stock that does! All of mine are specially bred to make use of high-technology lighting devices. You just need to get some uptown horses!"

Two days later, and I'm back at South Camp. Slim is chomping at the bit to relate that twenty minutes subsequent to departure of the previous pack train, his contemporary was horseback and burnin' leather for Hawk's Rest and the shortwave!

Following the next round out to the trailhead, I'm back in Peyton Place. This time proclamations are that all of Billings' hands are using flashlights and that that idiot is running four strings of high-tech mules in the Thorofare!

Shortly thereafter, upon a spruced-up Kelsey returning to town for a few days' R and R, he walked into the Silver Spur. Rumor has it that he had some real fast-talk explaining to do when the entire Judiciary Committee confronted him with his alleged and verifiably repeated use of a flashlight on the trail.

# Chapter 13, Bear Spooked from Texas

Early on in the career as outfitter, there was a series of phone calls from two fat guys out of south Texas. They related that they had successfully hunted for whitetails on several occasions and now wanted to give elk hunting a try. I detailed the nature of the trip into camp and tried to give them an idea relating to what they could do in terms of preparation. Remarkably, I failed to ask them about personal weight. So, with full details yet unexplored, the concerned was quite surprised when the pair showed up the night before, weighing 275 pounds, apiece. The hired hands simply shook their heads in disbelief. To add salt to my ineptitudes in the communications department, both of the hunters, whom we'll call Jimbo and Larry, told all of us that they'd lost 100 pounds, apiece, via an exercise regimen rivalling a daily rendition of the Bataan death march, coupled with starvation rations, in preparation.

Well, enough of ethnocentric considerations. It was time for horseflesh, and fortunately we possessed an ace in the hole. The saving grace was that the time frame was amid the early years, and so a significant portion of the fall stock consisted of lease horses. These had turned out to be quite good that particular year, and there were two big, stout, gentle ones, named Elmer and Gotcha. We had used them extensively the prior two seasons, so their reliability was well established. Further, I had two more of similar nature in the outfit dude string. These were Ky, a 16.2 Paint gelding, and Dick, a 16.0 hand Morgan. All four weighed in the vicinity of 1250, maybe 1300 pounds. Altogether, this trip, there were four hunters, three of us guiding, the wrangler and cook. This was the final outing of the season, and by that time, substantial accumulations of snow lay on the passes and at camp, as well. So, the plan was to double up on horses for Jimbo and Larry. Ky and Dick would take them from the trailhead to the top of the Deer Creek Pass, with Elmer and Gotcha trailing along empty. Then on the backside, we'd switch saddles to the empty horses, and go the rest of the way to camp, trailing Ky and Dick.

Well, originally there were a few doubts, watching those boys get mounted, but actually, they turned out to be pretty agile, and by the end of the day all were in camp, with no sore horses. Miracle, everyone thought. Perhaps the next miracle would be they'd both lose another 75 pounds over the next eight days before we had to take them back out to the trailhead!

That night, after supper, I held the usual short briefing regarding safety, firearms and bears. This was just some short, commom sense stuff, yet it seemed that after dark those Texas boys really changed. They seemed reticent to venture any distance from either the cook tent or their own sleeping tent. They asked if they should take a rifle out to the commode, and what if they ran out of firewood in relevant proximity to their stove? Most importantly, what if hunger struck at midnight? We all offered solutions, but it was apparent that these two were somewhat out of their comfort zones, and would probably require special attention from time to time.

Well, time to time came sooner than later!

Meanwhile, shortly after the meeting and with the stock fed and turned up the creek, bells aclangin', we hit the rack. It was late and cold October, the snowstorms tending to move in a couple times, daily, and so the whole place was frosted up. We were all a bit tired, worn from the long summer and fall seasons, a couple thousand miles horseback, and so it was very easy to recline and rest. However, one never really sleeps up there: just sort of, with an eye and an ear open, at least part way. You're listening for aberrant vibrations, or the absence of horse bells, (panic!) or bear sounds at the meat rack, mebbe the elk moving on the ridge above camp. Of course, there's always the symphony, or maybe an old screech owl, hoot-hooting around Halloween. Or, the Canadian honkers flying over, announcing that the elk migration is about to begin. How can anyone possibly sleep through all of that ... ??

Well, dozing probably around the time the bars in Jackson close, I'm guessing, when damned if those Texans aren't squawking about something. Their tent is now lit up like some kind of Halloween prank torch: a strobe-light combination, the beams rotating about the central axis of the structure. Baffled, it's time to get up, pull on the boots and stomp on over there. What the hell? But just then there's a couple of metallic clicks, and it's probably time to rethink the notion of intrusion. So, discretion proceeds back to reclining with both ears and eyes fully engaged. It seems the ritual proceeds awhile and then finally winds down.

A few flareups later, and I was thinking perhaps there was

more unawareness in the communications department, as in Crow Nation.

About two hours later came more squawking and a few SOS's, but when again I arose and went stomping on over, there were just rattling noises and wood going into the stove sounds, so rather than intrude and wake up the whole camp, better to return for rest and relaxation for the last spell prior to the witching hour. Fortunately, that went rather well with a bit of dozing, so 'long about 5:00 AM, it was time to light a fire in the dining tent and wake up the cook. That went alright as well, but 'long about thirty minutes later, the two Texas guys showed up, minus most of their clothes, and with quite huge double circles below their bag eyes. It was clear that neither had slept one iota, nor was either reluctant to relate his victimization story.

Well, as the temperature was running about 15 F. that time of the morning, there was concern that these two, clad only in their skivies, might be stressing over the extent of discomfort. Not so. Both launched into what amounted to a lengthy dissertation relative to the hazards of and remedies for thin-walled sleeping quarters in Thorofare bear country.

For a solid fifteen minutes, I was held virtually speechless over this incredible misadventure. To this day I cannot recall which one of these birds started the narration, let alone which one finally concluded it. However, within a few minutes of commencement, the whole camp was awake, standing bleary-eyed around two lightly and skivy-clad, wide-eyed fat guys telling their incredible story.

So, after playing ignorant and asking them how their night went, I shut up and tried to listen.

"Not good, sir ... . There was a bar outside our tent the whole night!" Larry reported.

"Yeah, and we heered him stalkin' clear around, yonder, and he cut loose with a deafenin' roar, a number a times. We wuz skeered!" Jimbo added.

"Oh?" I asked.

"M hm!  So we buttoned up our tent, tied up the entry, and built a big far in our stove ... packed 'er full of wood and opened the damper wide!" Larry explained.

A blur at best, here is the scenario in mind's eye:

*Snap ... crack.*

"Jimbo, you heer that?!"

"Yeah, sounds like sumpin' is out yonder, down by the creek."

"M hm ... and comin' closer. I'm thinkin' it's one of them bars they wuz talkin' about in the cook tiant."

"Definitely comin' on in ... . We better hole up. Quick, let's tie up the flaps of this here tiant."

"Eeee ... breeee!! Bre ... bre ... bre!!"

"Hell almighty, Larry! That's got to be the meanest, nastiest, snarliest grizzly north of the Mason Dixon and west of the Mississippi!"

"Get the rifles, Jimbo! We'll load 'em up with rounds chambered."

"I'm not messin' around with no safety!"

"Me naither!"

"You got the bullets, Larry?"

"Hell, I thought you packed 'em!"

"Well, let's not be messin' around ... . There, the flaps are tied, so no easy entry!"

"Hell, Jimbo, the goddamned bar isn't going to give a rat's damn whether the fliaps are tied. I heered they'll just walk in whar' they wants ... the front, sides ... all's the same to them."

"And he'll have you fer fixens, Larry, afore he gits to me!"

"Let's grab these sit down stumps this crazy outfit thinks is furniture, and use 'em to barricade the door ... . Come on help me roll these over and we'll stack 'em."

"Ok, but what if he tries to come in the side of the tiant?"

"A goddam bar isn't goin' ta come in the side ... he'd have to rip through all that canvas, plus he wouldn't be able to see whar he was goin', in the dark and all."

"Alright, Larry, we got to quit arguin' and tend to business. This is goddam serious!"

Snap! Clump, clump.

"You hear that?"

"Yeah!"

"He's right close ... we've got to build up the far! If we git the stove a rip-roarin', and the pipe outside the roof aglowin' ... I've heered that bars are skeered of stuff like that."

I'm shaking my head, wincing ... thinking it's lucky they haven't burned down even the winterized forest by now.

One of those fat boys, I'm thinkin' it was Jimbo, commenced with more 'splainin', looking at me with wide-open eyes.

"Yeah, let 'er rip. We figgur'd that would skeer the bar away, but we still kept hearin' 'im, crunchin' around in the snow, even right next to the tiant!"

"So, we rolled all three a them sittin' blocks over to the door-way and stacked 'em up, one top t'other."

"That way, we figgur'd if the bar tried ta come in, he'd hit the barrier, and 'bout that time we'd be ready with two full boxes of 'munition which we'd throw into the stove with the points aimed at the door!"

"That, plus our raifels loaded ... we'd make short work of that bar!"

"*Now yer finally makin' sense, Larry! Here, throw these hunks of lodgepole in that thar stove and set the damper to wide open! We'll freight train that bar clear outa the country!*"

"*Here's the ammo boxes, Jimbo ... .*"

"*Ya know, Larry, we might could use these as our second line of defianse ... like we could git ready, and if the bar comes in, breaks down the barrier ... we'll toss a box or two into this fired up, rip roarin' stove, with the points aimed at the bar. When she kerbooms, some of them paints is bound to connect, don't you think?*"

"*Damned shore should, Jimbo! Let's give 'er a try. We'll keep that third box of six-gun ammo in reserve, just in case he gits through the first barrage ... !*"

"*Plus, Larry, I'm fer loadin' these here raifels and havin' them handy, just in case the bar survives all the artillery. I've heard they're pretty damn tough!*"

"So, how did that work out?" I had asked.

"Well, it worked fine for a while ... but just about the time the place started to cool down, back came Mr. Bar," Larry answered.

"We went back into action, bullets ready and wood in the stove. We even had our hunting knives laid out handy. It got so damnable hot in that infernal tiant that we had to peel most of our clothes!"

"Yeah, every time we'd fire up the stove, seemed like the bar would leave, but then just as soon as the far started to burn down, back the sonofabitch would come," Larry declared ... .

"*Larry!*"

"Yeah, Jimbo?"

"It's gittin' powerful hot in here ... I'm playin' hell. We've got to cool this place down afore we git aphixiated! ... . What say we open the fliaps fer a piece?"

"No, we cain't! That bar'l see us and come on in, uninvited. We got to stay buttoned up!"

"Wal I ain't heerd hide nor hair of that bar ever since we last fared the stove ... ."

"Let's just let the stove cool down some. She'll burn out, and then we'll cool off."

"Alright, but I'm goin'ta have to peel some of these here clothes afore I die in this Godawful inferno."

...

"Finally, she's coolin' down in here, Larry!"

"Yeah, almost can't stand this Death Valley. Ya know, Jimbo, I wuz once in Furnace Creek when I wuz a kid, in California that is. My dad took all of us thar on a vacation when I wuz in high school. Temperature wuz 121 degrees in the shade, and that wuz extreme, even in Tiaxas. We couldn't git out of thar fastest enough! Headed back to Tiaxas early in the morn and were back home, night of the next day. Pops drove straight on through and never once stopped save fer gas."

"I'm thinkin' the same 'bout this place, pardner!"

"Yeah!"

Crack ... crack, snap! ... Clomp, clomp.

"Listen!"

"Dammit, Larry, it's the bar! ... and he's comin' back!"

"Hell's bells, and you wanted to open the fliaps!"

"Wal, then it's either the bar or aphixation! ... You got them bullets ready?"

"Yeah."

"I'll grab more wood, and I'm crammin' this stove full!"

"I'm thinkin' we better start conservin' on the wood supply, Jimbo. We're startin' to run low, and headed for high and dry ... as in a couple of sittin' ducks!"

Larry's voice suddenly jolted me into the present:

"And after a couple of hours, our wood supply was down to zilch, so we had to snatch the ridgepole brace," he explained.

"We got that sawed up into sections, with the meat saw, and

142

throwed all of it into the stove.  When the bar came back, though, the only wood left wuz from our bunks," Jimbo elaborated.

"Yeah, so we took those apart and sawed them up same as the brace."

"M hm, but by now the bar wuz circlin' our tent, closer and closer, plus he cut loose with one helluva beller, long about 3:30-4:00 AM."

"So, we really poured the fuel to the far.  We'll, this did no good, cuz the bar seemed like he wuz gettin' used to it all."

"Yeah, we wuz really gittin' desperate by this time."

"Finally, ever'thing just went all to hell ... and we had to start burnin' our clothes!"

"Trouble is, clothes either don't burn wail, or they just go up in seconds."

"Yeah, lak' when you tossed my new down vest through the hatch," Larry asserted, glaring severely at Jimbo.

"Wail, yer the guy who fared my wool britches and both pars of spenders, Jack Ass!"

The mind's eye goes berserk:

"Larry, it's the goddam bar ... again!  Every time we far the stove, he leaves; as soon as she cools down, back he comes!"

"This is damn shore gittin' old ... plus we're out of wood!"

"What?!  Now what the hell are we gonna do?"

"Hand me the meat saw, Jimbo.  This here brace fer the ridge pole has got to go.  We'll cut it into sections and throw them in the stove."

"How long 'til daylight, Larry?"

"Couple hours ... . I think most bars git outa sight once it gits light."

"Wal, in the meantime, what'r we goin' ta do 'bout wood?"

"Ya see them bunks we're sleepin' on?"

"Ya mean as in fuel?"

"You broke the code, Pard.  This fat boy wasn't born yester-day!"

"So, yer goin' ta give our bunks the same treatment as the ridgepole got? ... Whar in hell do we sleep, then?"

"It's two hours 'til daylight, pard."

"And what if we run out of bunks afore sunup, Larry?"

"Time to pull out all the stops and emergency burn the cloth-

*es and duffel bags, Jimbo!"*

*Snap, snap, crack ... Eeee ... br, br ! clump, clump, clump.*

*"Jimbo, he's really close, this time ... just outside the tiant! I'm throwin' the last of the wood from the bunks!"*

*"Toss me yer duffel bag, Larry!"*

*"Now just what do you think yer goin' ta do with that?"*

*"Start burnin' clothes, what else? Ya got any better ideas?"*

*"Not my clothes, you ain't!"*

*"So what would you druther, Larry? Cold or diad?"*

*"Wul, you kin burn yer own damn clothes, if you want to!"*

*"Hail, not that ... that's a brand new sixty dollar down vest, you sonofabitch!"*

*"Alright, Jimbo, next is yer elephant pant wool britches, and here's some goddam 'spenders that never did you nor anybody no good."*

*"Gimme those, you sonofabitch!"*

*"You Jackass!"*

By this time, there was a great deal of subdued snickering and under-breath comments among Slim, Kelsey and Dick. I was doing the best possible under the circumstances to keep a straight face, but finally couldn't, and the dam burst. Vibrating in amusement, I feigned shivering and invited all into the dining tent where the fire, this time, was pleasantly comfortable. Shaking their heads and rolling their eyes in disgust, the other pair of clients, muttering to themselves, headed back to their own tent.

In the meantime, it was starting to get marginally light, so time to grab a flashlight and go over for a foray around the disaster area. Within a few minutes, it was evident that there were no bear tracks, much less sign, but rather mule tracks from the camp pest, "Ol' Trapper." Over past seasons, he'd shown up, wandered into camp any time, day or night, looking for a handout ... as in horse cubes, bread or even hotcakes. Guess he figured that if he packed it in, he'd be entitled to some of it. Well, Slim came over, and we spotted the culprit lurking inconspicuously back just at the edge of the timber beyond the cook tent. We spread out and ran him back up the creek to where he was supposed to be. At thirty feet, and in a parting gesture, he threw a double-barrel at us, and brayed away back up the trail ... .

Back in camp, we got major problems. Two hunters and no

clothes! Further, both are big huge fat guys, and the rest of us are skinny. Nobody's got any extra clothes that will come even remotely close to fitting these two. I am absolutely at wit's end as to remedy.

Clearly, the two concerned are today not going to be getting much done in the way of hunting. Further, it's not sounding like either, at this point, could be pried away from camp, even with an eight-foot crowbar.

Meanwhile, over breakfast, the wheels are turning. It is surmised that maybe the neighboring camp, fourteen miles up river, might have a fat guy with a few extra clothes, and that we might be able to talk him into letting us borrow them for eight days. But then Kelsey reminds us we have two fat hunters in camp, and that one neighbor cannot be expected to provide viable remedy.

"Oh yeah, guess we better rethink this!"

Then there's the insurmountable problem of finding the words to justify such a request to some neighboring outfitter. Might prove to be too much to ask of a good friend. One could just hear it! "They did what?" Then I begin thinking about having to face all the stories and rumors that would inevitably turn up in every two-bit hovel from Cody to Cheyenne.

"Nope," I'm thinkin', "better keep this one bottled up, and handle it ourselves, in-house, so to speak."

So, we go to work. I've got an old, moth-eaten, multi-patched, wool shirt in the guide's tent, brought along for good luck and intended for emergencies. A couple of us help Jimbo get his big arms down the sleeves, which wind up barely reaching midforearm. The cuffs are splayed apart, so we tie them closer using a couple short lengths of baler twine. Of course, the circumference of the subject is quite enormous in proportion to that of the shirt, so the problem is addressed by lacing five-foot lengths of the same through all the button holes, wrapping the buttons and cinching the entire rotund works up proud.

Now Dick has a helluva pair of long-shielded welding gloves which he uses from time to time in the kitchen for handling hot stuff. He sees my eye on them, but that old-timer wasn't born yesterday, either.

"Not on my watch," he warns, his lantern jaw firmly set and the brow narrowed.

"But I do just happen to have an extra pair of rubber gloves, normally used for kitchen chores, but which, under the circumstances, I'll part with. After all, boss, I ride for the brand."

Then Kelsey, back from a foray to the guides' tent, manages to turn up a pair of wool liners, the likes of which were enough to kill for.

Well, so far, so good ... .

The two had managed, in their frenzy, to burn all their wool socks and a couple of their boots, so both were running on one wheel, so to speak. However, the second pair of gunners, in their benevolence, contributed to the cause with a pair of donated sandals they'd brought for relaxation in camp, and these we modified in combination with two pairs of Willy's wool socks, canvas and tear grease to create a semblance of size 14 footwear. We fashioned two "rights," as of course in the chaos, the concerned had trashed both right-hand boots.

Now we're making progress! Everyone in camp had gotten involved. We had to come up with some kind of britches, though. Well, Willy and Dick got to rummaging around camp and danged if they didn't come up with a couple pairs of old sweat pants, mistakenly left by a client on a previous trip. Unfortunately, they were a bit small, but no matter. Out came Dick's long kitchen knife, and damned if we didn't have two pairs, altered to size 60. Trouble was, they wouldn't stay up on our two hunters without one hand, apiece, holding them. Well, anyone knows that a gunner cannot accurately fire his rifle, one-handed, so if he gets onto the elk and decides to shoot, he's going to have to let loose of the trousers. So, theoretically, down go the trousers, and kerboom, down goes the elk. However, most likely, an old bull elk, about to bear witness to an imminent such spectacle of his own demise, will pour coal to the fire, and haul ass as in skeedaddle. No self-respecting critter would ever be party to such degradation as all that!

So, time to contrive belts, suspenders or some kind of combination riggin' to remedy the fleeing elk problem. Willy headed for the tack tent and returned with several old, sweated-up cinches we'd discarded from the pack trips last summer. We lashed several together, and mein Gott it's long enough for a sixty-inch belt! Time to run it around Jimbo and cinch him up but good. We tied up the whole arrangement with baler twine and half-hitches. Well, it wasn't meant for a Hollywood cinema or a Broadway musical, but by noon the first full day in camp, we had both of our fat boys up and fully running!

Yet, in spite of all the well-intentioned and heroic efforts, it proved impossible to talk these two pole cats into leaving camp, much less into going hunting that day. First Slim, then I, tried our best to manipulate, then coerce, Jimbo and Larry into getting horse-back and heading back into Varmint Creek, where we knew there were elk. Nothing doing! They insisted on "breaking in" their newly found wardrobes and trying things out, as Jimbo explained as sort of a "dress rehearsal" for the real McCoy, which could possibly occur as early as tomorrow. "Well, ok," Slim replied. "Those elk aren't goin' ta hang around forever!"

So, the rest of the afternoon wound up being a dry run, with both practicing cinching up those belts around 60" sweat pants, first standing still, then walking and finally with rifles at the ready. What subject matter for a home video! Larry even made a practice "run," much to the amusement of "Old Dick" and all the hunters, out to the commode and back, returning to the amazement of all, in good re-pair, with equipment intact!

Finally, all the trial runs and dress rehearsals must have passed the test, for at supper that night, the pair informed the whole crew that all was ready. Larry even went so far as to make the claim that the two were as prepared for "tomorrow's adventures" as any Southern boys had ever been in the proud history of the Wyoming Thorofare!

Kelsey had recently filled one of his two gunners with a three-year-old dry cow, as they were hunting meat. They'd be leaving later the following morning to pack in the quarters, after foot-hunting the second client closer to camp. Consequently, Willy wrangled late that evening, pulling in just enough horses for Slim, me and our two gunners.

It had been snowing sporadically over the past ten days, so we were all anticipating the migration. So far, there had been just a trickle, filtering out of the park, so to say. We were thinking that one of those days the dam was going to burst and the country would be covered up with the critters. I was guessing we might could fill both those Texans with big bulls that would do justice to the Lone Star. So, Slim left camp with Larry, planning to move in on Varmint where that last bunch of Yellowstone elk had holed up, probably for

147

a day or two. Jimbo and I headed up a different trail, planning to head west and look over another migration route off of Cyclone Ridge. We figured that if the exodus began, we'd have no trouble ambushing a heavy-horned old-timer lining out on the trail to Jackson Hole.

Well, we weren't too far off the mark. We covered some pretty good ground that day, glassing the timbered ridges as the snowfall broke sporadically, and the fog opened up. Always intriguing perusing the black timber on such frosty mornings. The elk show in the dark recesses, and among the shadows and convolutions in the high parks. That day and the next the wapiti were clearly starting to move. It proved remarkable, bearing witness to the amazement of my client at this event, totally orthogonal to his home culture. Significant was the level of captivation, for by the time we returned to camp, long after dark that evening, all traces of bear phobia had evaporated in the winds we faced throughout the day.

Slim and Larry had encountered much the same throughout their episodes and offered similar perspectives relative to the extent of migration. With large numbers of elk on the move, the issue of residual human scent would no longer constitute much of a factor, so we decided to peruse the same drainages and country again next morning.

In the meantime, Kelsey's second hunter had filled, taking another cow, which they'd be packing into camp from upcountry.

Next day, Jimbo and I were on Cyclone, glassing across the wide gorge toward the park line. Abruptly we heard two shots, then a third, coming from the direction of Slim and Larry. Then we heard Slim's 308 going kerwhack, and I was sure he'd just finished off Larry's bull.

"Well, Jimbo, that's three down, one to go. Put one on the wall fer Texas!" It was clear that Jimbo was elated. His eyes told the story of excitement on behalf of a lifelong friend.

So, ok, we hunted until dark, locating a bunch of about forty head. We pulled a sneak right up to the park line, getting into cows, calves, spikes and raghorn bulls, but couldn't get on the old-timer. He'd winded us, and those big tracks led back into the park. Those codgers weren't born yesterday. We rode on back to camp, the breeze spitting snowy dust in our faces.

Got there just in time to unsaddle and join Kelsey, Dick, Willy and all the gunners celebrating Larry's five-point bull. Slim claimed he'd never seen such a horse! Must have weighed a full 1100 lbs. on the hoof! "Played hell just getting him rolled over for gutting!" So, we hoisted a few that night along with Dick's supper of elk tenderloin and hash browns. In fact, Dick even threw in some cake from the Black Forest for good measure!

Next morning, we wrangled early, picking up packstock to bring in the bull, plus saddle horses for Jimbo, Larry, Slim and me. The plan was to accompany Slim and Larry partway, enroute to the elk, then break off and hunt the Varmint Ridge. We'd be checking out some of the timbered country Slim yesterday had claimed held several groups.

Amid the frosty air and sunlit horse-breath steam, we gave salutations of "Adios Amigos." It was about 10 F. and a bit chilly for cowboy boots and blue jeans. An hour later, Jimbo and I'd reached the chosen venue, so we tied the horses and slid along the edge of the timbered parks, rifles ready. The elk were moving, alright, just about how Slim figured, and yep, there was a bull. We crawled around, using a couple of sparse trees for cover, trying to close the range and locate an appropriate rest for a steady shot.

I was fixated on that bull and whispering at Jimbo to get ready, when the foul scent about knocked us over. "What the hell?? Mein Gott!!" Jimbo was on hands and knees staring down at the ground, then at me, incredulous. He was turning red faced. I sneaked back to him, and speechless, he pointed to the tracks, a full set in the snow, 8" fronts, 12" hinds, and splotched with blood.

Jimbo was frozen, crimson complexioned with fear. The scent was overpowering, and it was beyond convincing that the owner of those tracks must have been too close, as in point-blank.

We waited fifteen, eyes lasering the landscape, 360. All was holding well ... thus far, so good, yet with Jimbo by then fighting both a case of the look-behinds and the jitters, all at once. He was mumbling quite a collection of unintelligibles, and there was absolutely no success with any part of attempting to resume the elk hunting. Finallly, the client wailed that we had to get back to camp, and that all he wanted was to get back to Tiaxas!

Well, so we backtracked the bar, determining to pick up the horses on the way, and the trail went straight to Larry's bull, where he'd feasted on the gut pile. There we found where Slim had gotten the quarters packed, with his tracks headed down to camp. When Jimbo and I finally made camp, Slim met us at the corral. He took one look at my client, and his grin told the story.

Later, at the hitchin' rails, he cornered me in private. "Boss, I ain't never see'd two more bar-spooked cases of the 'look behinds' in all my forty years of packin' and guidin' in these here mountains. And now I've got to saddle these two fat birds up and listen to their bellyachin' about bars all the way, thirty miles to the trailhead!"

Well, we put Gotcha, Elmer, Ky and Dick to work, next morning, and packed them out to the ranch. Slim said they never broke stride, the whole way, not even for a rest stop! When they hit trail's end, they jumped in their rig, spun the wheels, and in a cloud of dust headed for the Colorado line. They were neither see'd nor heered from again.

Facts be known, for three years, thereafter, we never received one single phone call from a new potential Southern client.

Was this embargo on cause of them two bar-spooked fat guys? Mebbe!

Chapter 14, The Prussian of Valhalla*

Back in early November of 1996, Valhalla called.

...

The snow reveals in places, profuse and scattered blood-letting, and encountered are several antlered carcasses, recently gored in the process of their indulgences. The stares seem to transcend the agonies of combat, lending insult to the shivers. Horrified and proceeding with trepidation, it is compelling to approach a distant maximum concentration relative to cataclysmic endeavor ... at far line of discernible sight amid the vortex of the concerto's greatest crescendos, currently in the making, a return to the Paleolithic and Cro-Magnon.

...

By the mid-nineties, and operating out of the South Camp, we used to pressure the park line a lot, a practice I backed off of in subsequent years. Nevertheless, the original thinking was that we could "steal" a few of those old-timers whom we might not otherwise have cashed in on, should one or two careless make the inadvertent error of forgetting where, exactly, the boundary line was.

Well, that notion was ill contrived from its inception. Never was there clear-cut evidence that any one of those savvy creatures failed relative to awareness concerning location of that line of demarcation. Enclosure and closure are key, and, partner, you can bet your last dollar that every one of those critters knew, with precision, where status was protected and where status was not.

Back in the 80's and 90's, it seemed to this naive greenhorn that the park elk sought better feed than what was endemic to their indigenous hideouts. Thus, the theory anticipated that throughout what generally comprised the early weeks of fall hunting season, the groups would circulate the territory on both sides of the line, evidently to gain periodic advantage of a somewhat-enhanced nutrition. Consequently, those of us guiding the September elk hunters gained an opportunity to become acquainted with a wider spectrum cross-section of older park bulls.

Now, this initial reference to a more latent operational period

*Valhalla: Norse mythology: The great hall of fallen hero warriors.

of early November is significant. The same is being related owing to the uniqueness of the late-season time frame, insofar that it would have been coincident with the final trail run by packtrain of that year. Even then, in spite of recent acquisitions of several strings of younger mules, we were still short of stock much of the time. Thus, when it came to the point that the season had progressed to an extent making imperative we retrograde the camps, standards required we make that loose-ends final run to ensure the camps were clear.

Back in those days, we still hunted the full season's duration through to the end of October, thus attempting to maximize profits by squeezing in one last trip, optimistically anticipating that the weather would hold off that final week. Such good fortune would facilitate our successful escape from the elements, thus lending providence to another bountiful winter spent skiing in the Jackson Hole deep freeze. Well, in short, some years we made it ... and others, we paid the price for coming up short in the weather conditions department, thus suffering starvation rations for a while.

Well, ok. Slim and I had come in that first week of November, bringing twenty head of empty packstock over Deer Creek Pass. Recollection is that we spent about six hours shovelling trail, thus breaking over to the windward side of the divide, from where there was smoother sailing the remaining eighteen miles down to camp. There we planned to tear out the remainder of the facility, assemble the final loads, rest the stock a day or two, and then depart with the whole works in another epic escape effort, should the weather go to hell, once again, in a hand basket. Optimistically, however, we figured that the pass would tolerate just about one more storm before she shut down for the winter.

That second night in camp was a restless one. After reorganizing gear, building and weighing out the forthcoming loads, tearing out the remainder of camp structures and equipment and tending the livestock, we threw together a supper of sorts, which Slim topped off with a large pot of his "end of the trail stew." It was end of the trail, alright, for relative to physical condition, it was clear that my own rattling carcass possessed not more than one more run short of requiring major overhaul. Although never complaining, Slim related as much concerning his own status. It had been one helluva long year!

That night, after filling the tanks with Slim's stew, we turned in early ... but got no sleep. Although evidently holed up temporarily in the lower meadows a couple of miles below camp, clearly a large contingent of the park herd was generally moving. It sounded as though an entire Friday night convention was in progress. Recent weather had partially cleared, and a three-quarter moon lent its spotlight aura of enlightenment to all those timbered ridges over- looking camp. The entire lower drainage was lit up, illuminating amid the terraced ridges, quite substantial groups of elk, linked to- gether by satellite members who perpetuated visual contact, thus sustaining the inertia. Profuse activity ended the fatigue, and the adrenalin rush ensured entry to the edge of the Varmint Creek meadows, where vibrations lent the greatest credence to locale of assembly. If it were time for laying down green, a good bet would have been the Friday night fights.

At the time, I engaged only briefly in the wishful thinking rel- evant to the hunting season which had recently closed.

...

Slim had opted out of the late-evening foray, preferring rest and recovery in response to end-of-the-year fatigue.

I travelled alone. There was, of course, abundant snowfall, but having melted, subsequently refreezing, it offered compromising vibrations simultaneous with one's travel. Thus, upon maneuvering the last few hundred yards, in the process of making a strategically advantageous, circuitous approach to the clearings, one had to tread lightly. A careless approach, failing to lend credence to the crunching of leather boots against crusted snow, could send an en- tire herd of hundreds, perhaps thousands, on a hell run to perdition. I had witnessed worse cases on occasion, generally on the winter ranges, when inadvertent errors of man had compromised familiar- ity and produced chaos. It became necessary to judiciously guard against any false moves by treading ever so prudently.

...

I recall checking the wind at that point ... coming head-on and abruptly chilling in the face. All a good omen and offering no sign of any compromising swirling pattern. It brings a pungent, per- vasive aroma of half-fermented, barnyard-like manure scent.

153

Remarkably, the demigods are bugling profusely; in fact, at times the commensurate frequencies and collective efforts are so vociferous that the vibrations become a virtual continuum. The emanations are akin to sounds achieved, on occasion, at high altitude by electrical storms pervading dark canyons ... the massive tremors contained and bouncing, reinforcing among the walls ... thereby producing the nonstop thunder of Valhalla ... . Memories surface, retrieved from former years, older venues and deja vous.

...

There had been "Pecos Bill," who carried a splendid six-point rack of antlers, and who vociferously entertained his entourage with unique concert and epic overtures ... and "Medicine Man," the ancient Patriarch, massive 1100-pounder who carried seven-point antlers, and who dominated, on an annual basis, charges of over fifty head of cows, calves and satellites.

...

This night, these seasonal herd bulls produce variable thunder in abundance ... and the three-, four-, and occasional five-toner bulls spar with alacrity for the duration of their convention. It appears as though they are in celebration ... of survival, perhaps, with man's attempts at predation, at least in part, drawing to a close. More credibly, however, the ceremonial offers the inception of a movement ... of the large herd out of the deep snow country and, subsequently, on a long and perilous journey to bountiful wintering grounds and the best of God's country in the great valley to the southwest.

Amazingly, the vociferous bugling continues for a significant portion of the night, and I sit undercover, spellbound, acquiring the intonations, filling up on the energy of perpetuity ... the antlers cracking together with the strain of combat, opponents goring their opposites at the demarcation of cultures. It is here that the energy is greatest, purest and refinely directed.

I meet the first Prussian* tonight. Through it all, and most penetrating amid the orchestra, a purity of six-toners dominates the amphitheatre of snow-and-ice-laden terraces. The pitches bounce among the towers, reinforcing to greater intensity among echoes, and at times unique, it seems as though the entire proceedings will

*Prussian history: Friedrich Wilhelm, King of Brandenburg, 1640-88, who built the National Army.

briefly halt, with the membership paying tribute.  It becomes, of course, imperative to gain visual sighting of this "Great Elector,"* the bull who could achieve six tones, so nearly two hours into the holdings forth, urgent and timely to proceed with judicious intermission and break cover, thus crawling on hands and knees to mitigate the compromising emanations of crunching snow.

Relative to this inceptive breaking cover position, it is apparent that the elusive Herr Grosser Kurfurst* is holding forth across the main drainage. A guess estimates variable and mobile distance to approximate a half-mile, perhaps, on occasion, somewhat farther. The temperature, owing to intermittent breaking of the cloud cover, appears to be dropping, somewhat, albeit slowly, thus approaching 15 F. Time to suffer, imperatively, in silence.  The moon, now haloed by sporadic periods of intermittent snowfall, lends a spiritually and oddly haunting character to that silence.  Keeping as low a profile as possible means wet gloves and iced-up, frozen denims.  Suffering, however, is circumvented by sheer sense of mission.

The process of gaining the creek boundary proves itself unusually delicate, as the procedure involves a surgical one with passage among quite substantial groups of cows, calves and spike bulls.  Given the near absence of breeze at this point, or for the brevity of moments, the intermittence of a slight entity, coming in, southwest, off the park, a finessed level of judicious and timely crouching produces an apparent gliding effect, in lieu of a relatively alarming orientation, toward the participant observers.

Thus, by means of a series of timed crawling, low profiling and otherwise efforts at maneuver, it becomes possible to gain creek's edge of the main fork.  Often and intermittently pinned down by the incessant alarm intentioned barking of alert cows, or the curious glances of panic threatening "teenager" spikes, the process requires nearly an hour, thereby driving the inception of Phase II to past midnight. At the crux of the maneuver, encounter with an old, gray lead cow produces temporary stalemate.  She is the epitome of brightness, alert and refinely laser focused on this intruder.  The lack of breeze sharpens her perception effort, reminder of the growing list of old-timer matriarchs, as well.

...

Progressively, the matriarch total had gained in its vitality to

*Herr Grosser Kurfurst:  The Great Elector.

155

include Brunnhilde*, who in the 80's led the exit of late-season migration from Yellowstone's southeast corner. Initially, her charges had numbered in the hundreds, and metamorphosed over the better part of a full decade, to several thousand. She had led the vast majority, travelling by night, timbering by day, to impunity offered by the refuge in Jackson Hole. Her low-casualty success record must have rivaled the statistics of near perfection, and given man's efforts at intervention, as in zealous hunting, proved themselves remarkable, indeed.

Throughout the same time frame, Brunnhilde's counterpart, Kriemhilde*, clearly pushing twenty years of age the last time one of our hands recalled sighting her, for over a decade of Novembers, led a substantial portion of the indigenous herds from our drainages to safety on the Shoshone and Greybull Rivers winter ranges. Kriemhilde had quite a following. Observation by us clearly established that once the groups began the aggregation process, she offered the primary initiating influences relating to chronology of sequential movement, route of travel, choice of rest stops and the timing of daylight exposure. Given the vulnerability of the groups owing to movement and resulting enhanced visibility to predators, those choices had major impact affecting survival.

On occasion, by the late '90's, given the November atmospheric impetus influencing annual movement, it became clear that this "old gray cow" held, throughout her tenure, quite some influence with the portion of the herd which, each late fall, migrated east. The primarily indigenous bunch numbered in the vicinity of 1000 members, and when conditions reached the threshold, key elements deferred to her lead. The enclave broke into several cohesive groups, moving somewhat independently, but connected, often times, visually by individual sentinels. Thus, the migration proceeded methodically, with sufficient evidence over a decade, plus, of observation, to support the notion of a semblance of central authority ... .

...

All the while the Great Elector is holding forth his amazing melodics and six-toners, punctuated by the intonations and sparring sounds of his lesser charges. It is apparent that the major contingency of upper-echelon demigods have located in relative proximity as entourage, and so, with prospects fading relative to catching any

**Brunnhilde and Kriemhilde: Norse mythology: These were Valkyries of the Nibelungenlied.

sight of quest's object, a crossing of the drainage main fork is imperative. Raising the glasses gains the better optimum intensity light which technology can access. With steam rising from proximate, discontinuous thermal emanations in the making among the creek banks, pervasion facilitates itself, marginally, and it proves just feasible to discern antlers and gray shapes sparring at the far side of sporadic parks, opposite the preferred crossing point. As the concentrated steam rises, vision fades, and the lifting and falling mists lend a severe, yet surreal character to the Wagnerian scene. Perhaps the Wagnerian "Twilight ..." will prove itself forthcoming.

"Die Wacht*" continues awhile in spellbound silence, amid the clamorous raking of sharpened weapons over the creek flow, and a few pathetic efforts at thawing frozen hands into useful manipulators ... . Now more bulls are showing in the far series of meadows, and the sparring becomes more frequent and intense ... metamorphosing into warfare. For a short while it seems as though most are holding forth, bugling, crashing antlers, groaning, agonizing, clattering rocks and breaking down timber. Now the six-toner lets loose, once again, and the cacophony suspends for the brevity of recovery. Thus, resumes the ritual, once more, proceeding to crescendo, recommencing to combat and fatal exhaustion.

Time to resume approach, repeating the process that has brought fruition relative to the cows and calves. In seconds, the two feet of icy creek pervades every semblance of dryness and well-being of this pampered human carcass, and there is suffering in abundance. By the time of extrication via the far-side marginal excuse of an ice-pervaded gravel bar, jaws are clacking so profusely that the intractable contemplation surfaces that such racket might well compromise relevant proceedings and send the whole tribe to hell and perdition. So, now for judicious preemption and concurrent resumption:

"Alright, cowboy, git over it!"

It is notable that the next phase of intrusion metamorphoses into a foray to the "warzone of Verdun.*" Enroute and crawling, I begin to encounter open sectors of violently churned up, overturned ground, some aberrantly and majorly devoid of meadow grasses, others timbered, well endowed with broken, shattered limbs, bows torn up, littering the landscape in pieces.

*Die Wacht: The watch.
*Verdun: Site of the 1916, WWI battle, Meuse River, Northern France.

Again, echoes amid the mists, the six-tones ... and then abruptly, more alarming, temporary silence.

Approaching tentatively, low profiled and shattered, the dark process continues, sustaining minimal inertia, and enters yet another venue of protracted bugling and combat. Traversing meadow's edge of dark timber brings visions of two mid-range bulls locked in combat, the midsections of both raked and letting blood. Through the obfuscations of rising steam and lightly falling snow, the surreal manifests a pair irreversibly locked, their tines bored and irretrievably jammed .... Horrifying, witnessing their exhaustion and the impending.

The concerto continues ... unabatedly driving what seems to constitute lower intonations, the bars offering more the character of funeral marches ... thus to honor the casualties and the extent of sacrifice. The mists, parting, offer up more shattered torsos and fractured Nibelungen*, and insidiously emergent, pervading the intonations, perhaps by this point imagined, of Siegfried*, resounding the bars of "Die Gotterdammerung*," in offering to the heroes.

Another six-toner ... closer, this time, and then longer silence.

More bulls are showing, now, amid sparse timber a hundred yards distant. Now fully mature ones, clearly elders, heavily antlered, obviously among the hierarchy of the herd. None are feeding, but, rather, staring intently, vectoring in direction of an intruder, yet seemingly under no alarm. Nevertheless, time to cease all motion and, amid rattling canines, assume snow's low profile.

... fifteen minutes are followed by a sequence of six-toners, amid rising mists, shadowed movement among thermal steam and a backdrop of dark timber. Not a sound among the hierarchy ... and tension's pervasive silence among the demigods lends credence that jaw-rattling threatens the threshold of running them all to chaos. Seized literally to the edge of paralysis by the cold, it's time to crouch peripherally to better cover ... accomplished more through the graces of benevolent luck than owing to any talents on the part of the practitioner, thus without undue anticipated alarm relative to the entity in question.

Another hour of circuitous maneuvering to gain proximity to the origin of Siegfried, and the intensity of blasts amid signs of ferocious combat are at the threshold of overpowering any semblance

*Nibelungen:  In Wagnerian opera, ref. circa 1200 AD, these were the Burgundian kings~450 AD.
*Siegfried:  Warrior king of the Nibelungen.
*Die Gotterdammerung:  Richard Wagner's Twilight of the Gods, or Siegfried's Funeral March.

of the lucid. Frozen hands cover the overwrought ears.

Waiting time, as in pinned down by eight or ten of the demigods, all heavily laden in the swords department. But even a short pause is now unthinkable, as Valhalla beckons the consumed. No choice ... got to ward off the Valkyries*, yet again.

Another pair of six-toners emanate from the mists, bracketing an interval ... and now the demigods are moving, perhaps twenty, or so, of the hierarchy ... lining out and pushing a hundred or more of lesser protagonists through sparse timber ahead. Within a full minute the ground is vibrating, as though the entire population is waking up, the gears starting to grind into action.

Another six-toner, and it's time for "on point." The clouds are parting, the mists fading, slightly, and the attenuated moon beam is achieving a level of marginal penetration, lending subdued shadows of opaqueness to minor clearings amid the forest. Seventy yards and more to the front, the lined-out demigods obliquely pass, displaying those splendid Nibelung racks. They move as silent ghosts, drifting obtusely, finally halting, then milling insidiously, in tacit anticipation of the forthcoming. Six tones. More silence ... and Siegfried appears at fifty yards, emerging, ghostlike, from an edge of snow-bedecked, new-growth timber. He turns diagonally front, focusing lasered vision on the intruder, and lays back an enormous rack of swords. Drop sabres frame the scarred face. He is uniquely blond, and the hard features lend credence to many a successful battle. Within seconds he evaporates with the rising steam.

Inside of forty minutes, all the rest have vanished, as well, leaving no further traces beyond the tracks of 1200, headed for the great amphitheatre amid the Tetons.

...

To this day, I am spine chilled, haunted by the steam rising and intermittent breath ... the steely, black glare of the Prussian, levying assessment on an intruder. The gaze is rivetting, defying rebuttal, contradiction and surreptitious avoidance. That stare sustains its indelible impression, laser burned into ubiquitous eternal cognition, yet with the passage of brevity, attenuating ephemeral moonlight and rising steam, all that latently remain are ghostlike apparition, fading mists ... and thin air.

.*Valkyries: The war goddesses of Wodin, Norse god of war, who sent them to battlefields, thereby for making choices of dead soldiers for Valhalla.

One event which occurred each fall was at the end of the season when we pulled the camps. This was a time in the progression of trips when all had culminated in tired stock, possible accumulations of grub and horse feed, frozen, iced-up tents, coupled with the likelihood of substantial amounts of game taken owing to the enhancements of migration. It seemed that, no matter the extent of preemptive measures taken relative to combating accruals, there invariably was an enormous amount of baggage that had to come out to the trailheads. Nevertheless, given the inevitable assembly of all of the above coming to one major loggerhead, the week-long event nearly always proved to constitute an adventure of epic proportions.

Approaching Deer Creek Pass, mid 1980's.

One such unforgettable event occurred in the fall of 1984. That year, we caught a major snowstorm throughout the third week of September. There were 39" of snow on the level at the North Camp. Of course, that initially created remarkable hunting success, and we filled our parties in both camps within a few days. On the way out, packing hunters, meat, and shovelling the leeward side of the passes which had accumulated six- to eight-foot drifts, it became clear that the resident elk herds were making irretrievable mass exit, as well. Clearly, some of those old-timers had come close to getting caught in there some years prior, and were fixin' not to revisit that scenario. Ostensibly, it was turning out that those elk possessed more in the way of grey matter than did their pursuers, namely yours truly, who had, back in February and good faith, scheduled four or five additional trips into the same country. Now what??

Well, we ran those trips, alright, undoubtedly setting records for lowest success ratios in the proud history of Thorofare, Wyoming. We limped along at 25 to 30%, hoping for some park migration to fill the void in our country. This, however proved to be wishful thinking, at least until the last week of October!

Now, of course, those increasingly unsuccessful were not the easiest to get along with, as no one had been counting on the aberrant early snow. So, in an effort to mitigate the extent of victimization of these poor whiners, I offered the worst cases a free trip in the late season. Well, that went over rather well, at least until they returned, and the migration kicked into high gear.

So, later in October, back we all went, on tired, worn-out stock, and with guides who were starting to see double, as in fatigue. It was snowing like hell, and the two passes we had to cross were really getting treacherous. Near the top of the initial one, we handed several mule trains over to the hunters, who held them while the rest of us went to work with the scoop shovels. It took us six hours to get over. Consequently, we decided to circumvent the second pass, opting for a more direct route on into the South Camp. We pulled in about 1 AM, three of us and twelve hunters. Thank God for Dick and Willy, who helped us unpack all 25 head of mules, feed and turn out the stock, then filled us full of hot stew and coffee.

Sometime that night, she stopped snowing, for we woke up next morning to clear skies and bitter cold. The thermometer outside the dining tent read -12 F. After breakfast, some of us went hunting on foot, finding it imperative to let the horses rest and recover, somewhat, for what we knew would be forthcoming.

Well, this recent storm and cold snap had sure crow-barred the log jam. The Yellowstone elk were now moving, showing up on the timbered ridges, and it seemed that every major park had either tracks or critters!  By evening of that first day of hunting, we had seven elk on the ground, several of them with big antlers.  Mein Gott, when it rains, it pours!  Next session, Willy and I worked 36 hours, straight, packing elk quarters back into camp, while over the next two days, Kelsey, Slim and another guide named Pete filled all the rest of the Davy Crocketts.  In three days we showed those gunners over three thousand head!  No more whining from that bunch.

By the end of the fourth day, all the hunters had filled.  We had ten bulls and two cows.  The meat racks were strained to the level of breaking, and it was time for discretions relative to bear issues.  It was also time to load up and make tracks for the trailhead, as in depart the premises.  Said another way, time for escape, lest we become permanent fixtures for the duration of winter.

Most hunters and some guides tend to want to pray to the elk witch concerning the endowment of snow, thus to serve impetus for migration.  I'm sure our bunch did their share prior to that trip.  But, as in all endeavors, mankind had better use at least some care in the "pray for" department.  As for us, that year, we subsequently caught all the snow requested ... and some!

By the afternoon of day five, a northwester was blowing in off the Trident, and the icy wind chilled everything and everyone to the core.  By dark, she was snowing hard, and some of us stayed up most of the night, knocking snow off the tents to prevent their collapse and envelopment under the weight.

So, it was decision time.  The hunters kept insisting that now that they had their game, it must be judicious to depart this paradise. I could not disagree, but thought it better to let the storm play out and the snow consolidate, before attempting an exit.  Under the circumstances, you really do not want to tempt fate by playing the card prematurely.  We were, as usual, short handed, and it did not bode well to risk, under adverse weather and limited visibility, attempting the passes and winding up failing.  Then one inherits even greater problems in having to retrograde with worn-out stock.  Far better to hedge the bet with settled weather and accumulations, before attempting what is at best marginal.

We had lots to get done, and the gunners gave a great deal of help.  There would be 26 loads of game, primarily elk plus several mule deer.  In addition there were 19 loads from North Camp, 11 more of hunters' and hired hands' gear, plus 16 from South Camp, frozen, iced-up tents, camp accessories, tools, garbage and horse equipment. Figuring in the 18 head of saddle horses, the total came to 90 head. However, we only had 71 animals. Any way you figure, it was going to be necessary to come back with about 20 head of packstock for the rest of it.

Well ok, we tore out the entire South Camp, made up the loads and at midnight on trip day eight, under clearing skies, built a rip-roaring bonfire right where the cook tent had stood. We ate breakfast, wrangled in the stock, saddled up and began packing. Good thing we had taken the trouble to dry out as much of the gear (esp. halters and leads) as possible over the past ten days, as in temperatures below freezing, most of it when wet becomes nearly impossible to work with! By 10:00 AM, we were on the trail with 70 head, hunters, camp gear, game, horses and mules headed for the pass. The outfit stretched for a half-mile behind my saddle horse.

We rode in subzero cold, stopping twice to build massive bonfires and thereby warm up. Some of the tired stock were perpetually trying to lie down in the, owing to altitude, ever-deepening snow, thus to roll and relieve themselves of ballast. So, no real rest for the wicked, keeping ourselves wound up hollering at the troublemakers.

Seven hours into the run, we hit the wall of wind-driven drifts about 500 yards short of the pass. Hell's bells, it didn't take long for snow to settle in and for the breezes to kick up. This one was coming in straight off the Tetons, the wind-blown, orange-glowing ambience evidenced by all of us at sundown. Clearly, by now, the howling was speeding along at 35 to 40 mph, and with the temperature down around zero, the chill factor was getting rather serious. No place for cowboy clothes in these parts! Blue jeans, tall boots and jumped-on hats?? Maybe on a Sunday afternoon on the Brazos ... but Deer Creek Pass in November!!??

...

Well, it's time to go for broke. We divide the strings into twelve roughly equal parts and hand them over to the gunners, precautioning them relating to the potential for getting trampled by overzealous, claustrophobic stock trying to blow the pop stand. Most of our hunters are steady Southern boys, well endowed with savvy and common sense. Thanks to the Boss for Texas and Alabam'.

The rest of us grab the scoop shovels and go to work. We shovel like crazy, flashlights in our teeth, and immediately are sweating in spite of altitude, cold, wind and dark. Periodically, it is compelling to go back down to the packs and check on the hunters. Clearly, they are catching hell's duty, trying to stay warm, given the conditions. I am met by wolves' eyes, blank stares and frosty packs, until finally someone shouts ... "How much further, Boss? ... are we getting close?"

At a loss for answers, there can be only, "Getting there ... ."

As daylight fades to black and the nebulous, visions appear amid the howling wind and snow ... the mules creating large shadows in the wake of illumination. They metamorphose and become elephant-like ... reminiscent of Hannibal's armies crossing the Pyrennes, enroute to Rome.

Finally, some of these gunners have got to be spelled off, so we build a fire in sheltered timber, somewhat out of the pervasive wind. In short order, we rotate hands and clients, three at a time, briefly, for warmup. Several of the guides are getting spent, as well, so we also send a couple willing gunners up to man the shovels.

Well, the rotation process appears to be working rather well, but in three hours, we've made less than 200 yards progress. Everyone, including both livestock and humans, seems to be more or less in reasonable frame of mind and holding it together.

Time to be contemplating the leeward side, if we get over, however. That's going to prove the ultimate test, proceeding to find the trail under twenty feet, let alone shovel it! The concern is that in wind, the leeward side cornices, and so, when moving out becomes imperative, one can never be absolutely certain that all are over terra firma.

That being the case, I head up there for a look-see, hollering encouragement to the shovelling crew, while passing them enroute. Their heads are down in the shadows, beyond the flashlights, and clearly they are working as demons possessed. One can only pray that their heroic energy holds out, for there are enormous hurdles ahead of us.

Snow now reaches neck level, and wallowing turns to swimming, as in muck, toward the summit. A hundred yards below the top, it's over my head, necessitating shovelling for several minutes to gain even two or three steps. What a fight! One sweats what seems like buckets trying to make the saddle. In twenty minutes, looks like to be about half-way, but upon turning around, all the work what got cut out minutes prior, has blown back in behind. Going to be a major fight, just getting back down to the outfit!

Finally, at the top, all there is is white! Can't make out the difference between fallen snow on the ground, and blowing snow above it. Starting to dissipate as to what's up, down, sideways, black or white ... all blending into fading. Mein Gott! At this point there is no clarity as to bearing relative to crossing point, much less a trail off of it ... all nebulous.

Under the circumstances, it is unconscionable to proceed on an organizational basis. The risks far outweigh the infinitesimal probability relative to success in getting over and free of this frozen, hellacious trap. With bitterness, it is concluded that continued effort in this direction now enters the realm of the irresponsible. What a mess!

Time to bail off the top and, shovelling most of the route back which now shows only inconsequential signs of initial ascending passage, fight a way to the shovelling crew. They're incredulous upon receiving word to meet at the fire.

Half an hour later, all the hands and about half of the clients are standing like scarecrows, reflections from the flames accentuating demonic expressions of exhaustion. They are drained but ironically grateful upon learning of the situation and that we would be returning to camp. The difficult maneuvering of getting seventy-plus head turned around and headed back down the trail, under present conditions and darkness, proceeds with neither complications nor disparagement.

...

Upon arrival at location, we unpack, tend to the livestock and roll out under our old favorite trees. With the familiar comes relief and exhausted, interminable sleep, leaving to the morning a better-focused vision concerning alternatives.

Chapter 16, Escape

Alternative pursuit, of course, constituted the only one prag-
matically available, a reroute out to Jackson Hole. It was, at least
for our sector of indigenous elk, the preferred and most popular alternative, offering prognosis, most years, for the best of feed and
relatively wind-absent winter months.

Among the full spectrum of years spent in these parts, I
never once considered, with trepidation, the option. Rather, it constituted a preeminent tradition, one which the wildlife willingly had
taken, apparently since well before the inception of any human
records relative to the matter. It was esteeming to somehow com-
prise a minor part of that precursor to paleolithic history, that is, to
achieve somewhat of a linkage with the herds which we, only a few
hours prior, had pursued in deadly earnest, thus ultimately becoming part of an entity much greater than ourselves, any human inter-
pretations of inconvenience and discomfort be damned. The option
represented entry through Hegelian notions of horizonal pursuits,
relative to transcendental passage, in terms of Aufhebung. As such,
it offered adventure, opportunity, perhaps even the ultimate test,
rarely, if ever, encountered in human life, much less forced upon
one's issues. Yet to forgo such privilege by opting out via contemplated, contrived or self-serving preferred options, would go beyond
conscionable levels of commitment, perhaps to a level synonymous
with treason, relative to that life, itself.

And so, time for a battle plan. We spent the next couple of
days hanging gear, saddles, pack covers, lash ropes, and so on, in
direct sunlight off hitching rails or anything else horizontal that was
available, thus drying out most of the equipment. Stacks of frozen
halters and lead ropes set in proximity to bonfires hastened the
process. The timing coincided with resting the stock, all of whom
seemed to relish the time being turned out in the lower meadows,
in conjunction with their feed being augmented by the remnants of
remaining horse cubes. All of us worked on gear by day, reorganizing the packs and sleeping amid moonlit, cloudless and very cold
nights. Finally, all was made ready, and by midafternoon of trip day
11, we had collected quite large quantities of fuel, and proceeded
with building a pair of enormous bonfires for the ritual.

By dark, all the packstock were saddled, the final four bags

166

of cubes being distributed, and we went to work on the loads. Thank the Real Boss for dry lash ropes, well-fed stock and diamond hitches.

That final trip we hunted the high ridges with abundant success.

Around midnight, the job finished, we pulled tight the cinchas, latigos and adjusted quarter straps, departing camp with four strings of twelve, each, mules and packhorses. There were eighteen saddle horses, plus a few spares pulling up the rear.

The temperature must have been pushing -20 F., for just prior to the crossing point at Badger Creek, we could hear the loud cracking and creaking of the ice.

Well, in spite of our layered clothing, and hours of burning calories prior to departure, it was not long before everyone was suffering a bit. Any concept that humans, cowboy or not, derive the benefits of transmissible body heat by virtue of sitting horseback, are ill founded. The cold, even without wind, and despite a certain dryness, thereof, here in the West, in short order becomes pervasive, invading every extremity, covered or not, layered or likely not, and becomes venomous to the cores of existence. A continual invective torture dictates a suffering over the long hours and miles, and, in our circumstance, there were forty-seven such miles to cover in the process of achieving the opted-for trailhead in Jackson's Hole.

So, part of the remedy, if one is to make progress under the circumstance, lies in, from the inception, abandoning any faith that, somehow, the trusty steed will at some point benevolently turn up the heat register and provide relief. Alleviation and ultimately preemption comes from abating one's loyal companion of the extra ballast, thus opting for self-imposed inertia on the part of the rider, that is, in lieu of restful stagnation. In any event, and with variable snowfall piling up, one warms up rather quickly. With judicious alternating of the two activities, riding and walking, and a bit of experimentation relative to the extent of indulgence in each, a tolerable balance can be achieved, thus mitigating the attenuating effects to a level of endurable suffering.

Late season success at North Camp, just before the big storm.

Well, ok. This works out fairly well until it's time for a swim at one of the local spas, that is, one equipped with neither heat nor steam, as in fording the Thorofare River. The locals, as in wildlife, claim the process must be brief and can prove itself invigorating.

So, having played the game a few times prior, it loomed judicious to approach with a degree of caution. Ice on relatively large bodies of water can prove itself tricky, offering variably and questionably sustainable support to eleven-hundred-pounders on four legs, coupled with death-by-drowning undercurrents for surprise consumption by the unaware, beast or man. Consequently, it's time for a halt at the bank, for breaking up the strings and allowing the stock the specific choice of route, thus avoiding catastrophic mass destruction owing to naive "sharing of the wealth," so to speak.

We all dismount and proceed to lead our gallant steeds across the narrows. At best the episode is nerve-wracking, leading all through an icy, snow-laden maze of broken, crystalline structure, melting, somewhat, by day in sunlight, rebreaking and then resolidifying amid the coldness of night. Frozen, iced-up and frosted circumventing vistas lend starkness to an opaque, glowing austerity amid creaking, screeching emanations of the giant icepack, now groaning under the shifting weight of tons of horseflesh, and seemingly on the verge of giving way to swallow the living into the black vortex of voracious, suicidal waters. Finally, the nerves achieve the limit, and I halt, briefly, waving and hollering to outrider Willy, to hold the second half on the back side of the river until the already committed can safely pass. Minutes later, we come face to face with the black demon: open water glaring back, daring us to proceed. Bandit snorts abruptly, glaring first at it, and then at me with, "Now what, you idiot?"

We find a way around the fracture, assimilating the ominous cracking and splintering throughout the detour, as mule hooves threaten penetration and shattering of the structure, and thus impending and decisive destruction.

Finally, we emerge, drifting with clacking shoes and balled-up ice out onto the snow-absent thermal rocks of a far-side gravel bar, everyone within the first string intact. Gott sei dank! Second string appears, shortly, coming in through the mists and following in our tracks, arriving minutes later, unimpaired. With the flashlight, I give the prearranged high sign to Willy to come with the rest.

Ten minutes later, profound relief. In the moonlight and frost, we count the vapored breaths of the last thirty head and human counterparts. Next to get the clients horseback, loose stock ordered, retied and lined out. Good thing those seasoned hands had presence of mind to tie those leads up short. Left long or even marginally beyond diminutive, the act of drinking produces saturated, then impossibly frozen halter ropes. So much for all those efforts at drying them out back in camp!

We drive on down river, until, an hour later, reaching the Yellowstone Meadows. The whole monstrous amphitheater is lit up, sparkling away, silvery, the terraced grandstands surrounding us in magnificent moonlit splendor. We encounter herds of buffalo at close quarters, among them bulls of enormous size, who, as though irritated by the intrusion, with curved horns and sinister expression ominously glare at our procession. In no moods for confrontation, we unobtrusively pass, circumventing with silence potential encounter, the surreal images fading amid the timber and among the mists. An incisive howling of coyotes frames distant echoes of far-off honking Canadians, crossing a nearly full moon. Amazing how luck among the living accentuates the latent hour, thereafter ... in living spectra and polyphonic echoes.

Rest stop in the cold.

We ford the Yellowstone, which, owing to the pack bridge

and diminutive waters, is cake. No need to split the strings ... just a couple of broken lines owing to unfamiliarity among the few uninitiated with the structure, and a reticence to become acquainted. Driving on, new adventures loom, as in unavoidable swamp ice, bilge waters from beaver dams purposefully emplaced to provide harassment to midnight packers trying to escape Thorofare wrath in November. So, danger ahead. Time to split them up!

"Tie those leads up short and sweet, gents!"

We blast on through, in the wake of what looks to be frozen tracks of another outfit. The broken-up, refrozen ice is more treacherous than anticipated, and several of the packstock are down in four feet of muck. Three of us are off our mounts, proceeding with rescue. An invigorating icy episode, pulling packs, cutting latigos, retightening cinches and throwing diamonds in all the mess. All of us are cussing the beavers and the god that created them.

Inception of a late season Thorofare escape episode.
With pastern-deep snow at camp, the high passes often became horrific.

In spite of our cussing and damnation of the beaver creator, the Boss smiles and at least temporarily forgives our trespasses and sinful indiscretions, only to throw us a blindside curve at the forthcoming mouth of Atlantic Creek. Here we hit more work of the

171

log-jamming beavers. This time it's several hundred yards of black ice, where the creek has overflowed the trail, plus it's got us channeled owing to massive boulders and timber preempting circuitous rerouting. In short, we are locked in and confined to a sidehill-exposed black-ice trail. There is no visible, much less imaginable, remedy.

"Git off those horses, and cut the packstock loose!"

So, we proceed up this goddamned rat-slick excuse of a trail, groping for handholds, leading our falling-down, soon-to-be banged-up saddle horses, and what packstock can be lent a hand. Within minutes, everything and one are falling down, sliding into rocks, timber, horse and human flesh, tearing up the packs, cursing the blue out of darkness, creation and more. What a rat f...g chaotic mess! For what seems an eternity of infernal nightmare, we curse each other, mankind, ourselves, the heathen fools who originated such contrived adventures, and creation, itself.

Twenty minutes later, about ninety percent of all are somehow standing on terra firma, having managed to stumble through all the mass disorder. Then Slim hollers that we've got six head down and jammed at the last corner, and that two of the hunters are piled in with them. By the time several of us reach the action, Kelsey and Dick have succeeded in pulling the clients free of the wreck, and the same are unhurt. The stock are fully tangled amid blowdowns, lash ropes, packs and gear. We jump in and start cutting lines, the effort made to free the animals from entanglements with misarranged gear, which threatens to strangle them. A couple of the packhorses are coughing up blood, and on one it looks bad, as in frothy and dark. He is going crazy, run partway through by the lodgepole blowdown, owing to the forces of the wreck. Willy offers the sideways glance, and I nod concerning the obvious. Kelsey and Slim lend a hand to "off the trail," and the lever action ends the agony. We are numb over the tragedy, yet the injury to the second is apparently less threatening.

He's not lung-skewered, but has majorly bitten his own tongue, owing to all the thrashing around. There's blood all over the landscape, as he's nearly severed the object of investigation. We powder him with blood coagulant, using nearly a full can of the stuff, plus load him up with butanol. He'll make it, empty, of course, so time to bring up two of the spares, refit saddles, gear and repack.

The Texans build us a good bonfire, and we proceed to refit the six head.  Gear is majorly torn up, so out come the baler twine, spare leather, duct tape, tools and rivets.  Our hands are nearly useless, given the cold and incidental exposures owing to the wreck.  All are constantly trying to reinvigorate them via multiple trips to the fire.  Thank the Boss for the Alabams who now hold the packstock intact, while we work on repairs and repacking.  In two hours, repacked, baler twined, wired and rivetted together, we are off the incestuous ice and back on the trail, terra firma.  For the moment I am profoundly exhausted, owing to the loss of a favorite.  It's affected Willy, as well, who had mumbled the same to Slim at the fire.  Riding for a while helps, allowing resilience to take effect.  It's starting to get light.  There is silver on the horizon, back east, beyond the Yellowstone.  An hour later, and it's possible to make out the Thorofare River, and finally the lower end of our camp drainage.  Home sweet home, once again, next summer.

"Auf Wiedersehen, mein Freund."

The enlightenment by day elevates the spirits, some, noticeable concerning Slim and Willy, riding behind.

Just before sunrise, she turns more bitterly cold, typical of mountain air, achieving concentration just before the sun's rays attenuate the density.  Must be about -25 F., and the extremities are protesting.  Time to get off and walk.  Clearly, Slim and Willy are indulging the same.

By late morning, we've come the rest of the way up through the Atlantic Creek timber, and are starting to top out along what constitutes a widely separated series of long parks.  The timbered edges seem to recede into a nebulous, faded oblivion, now obfuscated by the mists and blowing snow.  The wind, once absent in the lower stretches of timbered Atlantic, has picked up amid higher elevations, and now threatens with increasingly prominent ice-laden drifts.  We fight a way through them, which offer the worst where the balkas emerge from lateral timber.  An hour later, we reach the barely perceptible high point, known to yours truly from the summer pack trips, where waters separate from a single source point, split into going east and going west, thus to the Atlantic and the Pacific ... "Parting of the Waters," at Two Ocean Pass.  In summers the place is full of tall green grasses and abundant wildflowers, a paradise for horses and wranglers.  Today, it's austere, wind-blown and nearly unfit for visual processing.  Glancing backward, it's not possible to ascertain anything beyond midway of the pack trains, as the remainder are faded by winded snow and the mists.

Another hour, and we've clearly made the head of Pacific Creek, fully terraced and frosted from head to foot.  A substantial herd of elk, perhaps 150 head, has holed up in the wind-free upper basin.  They eye us warily from 800 yards, and soon drift into dark timber.

Clearly, they're on the way to winter ranges, as are we.  Remarkable that some showing up on the wintering slopes have been traced from as far off as middle Thorofare, Pass Creek, for instance, some 70-plus miles distant from the refuge.  Notable that diligence of effort ultimately leads to delicacy, in reference to palate, augmented by the enhancement of setting.  We cross Pacific Creek, amid dark waters of substantial depth, as in 4 feet.  The stock breaks through thinly layered ice, and everyone is awash in frozen slush.  Quite invigorating with sk's, straw hats and denim.  "Gott sei dank," for longjohns and wool!

Thorofare splendor in November.
This was just before we pulled out to Jackson Hole.

Time to grab the cutoff to Trail Creek Divide, which will lead us over the top and into the North Fork of the Buffalo River. Owing to the big wash at Pacific Creek, the folks are begging for a rest stop and a fire. Sounds good, so long as we build a rip-roaring one. We separate the packstock, tie up in dense timber, and kick back. Those Southern boys sure are handy at finding fuel and putting it to good use! They have two well started before the rest have finished with the stock. Time to join this glass-eyed bunch, now looking a bit stressed and tired, yet given a few words of confidence, they come to life, asking how far we've come and how long yet to go. "Too far and not long; after all, we're on the road less travelled, or more accurately, the road last travelled."

"So, we're the last ones out of here?"

"Naw, not out of here, but from the Thorofare, yes."

Well, ok. We hang out and thaw for an hour, then it's boots and saddles. Another hour and a half, and we're off the switchbacks and in the North Fork. The Tetons are locked in afternoon alpenglow mist, reflecting an ambience unique to the valley. We push groups of elk ahead of us, joining the timeless ages of their rituals, enroute. Remarkable that the mule deer seem to be traversing orthogonally, opting for obtuse migration routes in near opposition to those of the majority of elk numbers. Many appear to originate in eastern Idaho and northwestern Wyoming { Teton Region }, then traverse the Atlantic Creek, Yellowstone and Thorofare River country, finally for the winter months winding up far to the east of the Continental Divide, on the Shoshone and Greybull River watersheds. Even Mother Nature at times perplexes the naivete' of those lesser endowed among us, with such baffling renditions of dyslexia.

We cross the forks of the Buffalo River. Fifteen miles to go!

We ride the final miles amid the second-cycle hours of our dark epic. Likely those Southern boys are so numb by now that there's not a complaint left in them. At least there's no sign of any. The stars are fully out, and under cloudless skies, we travel into the void under constellations set apart by showers of meteors and an unusual brightness of galaxy, accentuated by the substantial coldness. Amid imaginary shadows of the Tetons, time seems to stand inert. The saddle horse plods along, keeping time with the stillness, on an endless march from a timeless place.

We pull into the corrals at Turpin Meadow a couple hours

prior to midnight. It's absolutely pitch black, but there is light in the faces of the riders and in the eyes of our horses. Those who are able lend a hand, help us unpack, stacking gear and game in long rows for loading on the trailers and trucks. The stock we leave saddled, with cinchas looser, to ensure warmth for the long haul back to the South Fork.

In the meantime, the vehicles arrive, and we proceed to load them up. Another 340 miles and we'll mothball this colossus on the Shoshone, patching up the gear all winter for another go next year.

Ah, yes, and in this sleep-starved stupor, I nearly forgot. Got to go back with 20 head for that last set of packs we left in camp. Hope somebody is willing to go with, and that we'll not have to shovel the passes. Wishful thinking.

Hals und Beinbruch!

Wishful thinking ... that we'll not have to shovel the pass!

...

# and so, nearly 40,000 miles later ...

Well, Pardner, I hope you liked this book.

May you keep that old pedal to the metal,
...
and when amid them rattlers, grizzel bars

and kamikazes on the fly,

ne'r forget to keep yer powder dry.